REDISCOVERING the FORGOTTEN YOU

TAKE BACK YOUR PASSION, REIGNITE YOUR DREAMS, AND EMBRACE THE LIFE YOU WERE CREATED TO LIVE

JOEL OSTEEN

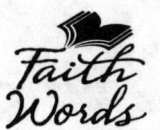

LARGE PRINT

Also by Joel Osteen

15 Ways to Live Longer and Healthier
15 Ways to Live Longer and Healthier Study Guide

All Things Are Working for Your Good
Daily Readings from All Things Are Working for Your Good

Blessed in the Darkness
Blessed in the Darkness Journal
Blessed in the Darkness Study Guide

Break Out!
Break Out! Journal
Daily Readings from Break Out!

Digest Books
Believe
Chosen
Excellence
Stay in the Game
The Abundance Mind-Set
Two Words That Will Change Your Life Today

Empty Out the Negative
A Fresh New Day Journal

Every Day a Friday
Every Day a Friday Journal
Daily Readings from Every Day a Friday

Fresh Start
Fresh Start Study Guide

I Declare
I Declare Personal Application Guide

Next Level Thinking
Next Level Thinking Journal
Next Level Thinking Study Guide
Daily Readings from Next Level Thinking

Peaceful on Purpose
Peaceful on Purpose Study Guide
Peace for the Season

Pray Bold

Psalms and Proverbs for Everyday Life

Rediscovering the Forgotten You

Rule Your Day
Rule Your Day Journal

Speak the Blessing

The Power of Favor
The Power of Favor Study Guide

The Power of I Am
The Power of I Am Journal
The Power of I Am Study Guide
Daily Readings from The Power of I Am

Think Better, Live Better
Think Better, Live Better Journal
Think Better, Live Better Study Guide
Daily Readings from Think Better, Live Better

With Victoria Osteen
Our Best Life Together
Wake Up to Hope Devotional

You Are Stronger than You Think
You Are Stronger than You Think Study Guide

You Can, You Will
You Can, You Will Journal
Daily Readings from You Can, You Will

Your Best Life Now
Your Best Life Begins Each Morning
Your Best Life Now for Moms
Your Best Life Now Journal
Your Best Life Now Study Guide
Daily Readings from Your Best Life Now
Scriptures and Meditations for Your Best Life Now
Starting Your Best Life Now

Your Greater Is Coming
Your Greater Is Coming Study Guide

REDISCOVERING the FORGOTTEN YOU

Copyright © 2026 by Joel Osteen

Cover design by Micah Kandros

Cover image © Shutterstock

Cover copyright © 2026 by Hachette Book Group, Inc.

Hachette Book Group supports the right of free expression and the value of copyright. The purpose of copyright is to encourage writers and artists to produce the creative works that enrich our culture.

The scanning, uploading, and distribution of this book without permission is a theft of the author's intellectual property. If you would like permission to use material from the book (other than for review purposes), please contact permissions@hbgusa.com. Thank you for your support of the author's rights.

FaithWords

Hachette Book Group

1290 Avenue of the Americas, New York, NY 10104

faithwords.com

@FaithWords /@FaithWordsBooks

First Edition: April 2026

FaithWords is a division of Hachette Book Group, Inc. The FaithWords name and logo are trademarks of Hachette Book Group, Inc.

The publisher is not responsible for websites (or their content) that are not owned by the publisher.

The Hachette Speakers Bureau provides a wide range of authors for speaking events. To find out more, go to hachettespeakersbureau.com or email HachetteSpeakers@hbgusa.com.

FaithWords books may be purchased in bulk for business, educational, or promotional use. For information, please contact your local bookseller or the Hachette Book Group Special Markets Department at special.markets@hbgusa.com.

Library of Congress Cataloging-in-Publication Data

Names: Osteen, Joel author
Title: Rediscovering the forgotten you : take back your passion, reignite your dreams, and embrace the life you were created to live / Joel Osteen.
Description: First edition. | New York : Faith Words, 2026.
Identifiers: LCCN 2025049620 | ISBN 9781546005223 hardcover | ISBN 9781546005247 ebook
Subjects: LCSH: Self-actualization (Psychology)—Religious aspects)—Christianity | Self-realization)—Religious aspects)—Christianity | Christian life | LCGFT: Self-help publications
Classification: LCC BV4598.2 .O8674 2026
LC record available at https://lccn.loc.gov/2025049620

ISBN: 9781546005223 (hardcover), 9781546005247 (ebook), 9781546010975 (large print)

Printed in the United States of America

LSC-CRW

Printing 1, 2026

This book is dedicated to my mother, Dolores "Dodie" Osteen, whom I loved dearly. She was the matriarch of Lakewood Church, an amazing woman whose faith, courage, perseverance, graciousness, and sense of humor touched the world. My mother believed in the power of God's promises. She stood strong in faith, even in the most difficult times, and through her example she taught all of us to trust that with God, all things are possible. Every day of her life, she encouraged us to rise higher, to dream bigger, and to become everything God created us to be.

Author's Note

Before you were formed in your mother's womb, the Creator of the universe put in you everything you need to succeed, to overcome obstacles, to achieve your dreams, and to leave your mark. Too often these days, we let the pressures of life wear us down and we lose track of the person God created us to be. We forget that person and we get discouraged when things don't turn out the way we hoped, when people let us down, when we feel drained and out of strength. But remember, you are still exactly who He designed you to be. This is not the end of your story—God has fresh strength, new joy, and greater favor coming your way.

In this book, you will rediscover how to rethink and overcome challenges and discouragements that may be holding you back. You have abilities and potential that at the right time, just like a gene that's been lying dormant, will open, and you'll discover gifts you had forgotten were in you, and others that you never knew you had. It's easy to think that we've reached our limits. *This is the family I come from. This is my education. This is what I'm good at.* We look at what we've seen in the past, but what you can't see is what God put in you that hasn't been released.

You can't see destiny genes that haven't opened yet. When you come into an opportunity that looks over your head—to apply for a management position, to start a business, to teach a class—thoughts will tell you, *You can't do that. You're not qualified. It's too much.* But God wouldn't give you the opportunity if He hadn't already equipped you for what you need. The reason it feels over your head is because there is talent, courage, favor, and skill that you have forgotten—and others that you haven't seen yet. It's all in you. As you take that step of faith, you'll rediscover that you've already been programmed to do what God is asking you to do.

I heard about a minister who handed a man a hundred-dollar bill before the church service and asked him to secretly put it in his wife's Bible. During his message, the minister asked the woman to stand up. He asked her to trust him and then to open her Bible and give him the hundred-dollar bill inside it. She shook her head and said, "I'm so sorry, pastor, but I don't have a hundred-dollar bill." He asked again, "Do you trust me?" "Yes, I trust you,"

Author's Note

she said. "Then please open your Bible and give me a hundred-dollar bill." Frustrated, the woman opened her Bible and much to her surprise, she saw the hundred-dollar bill. She looked puzzled and said, "How did it get there?" He smiled and said, "I put it there." That's the way God is. He'll never ask you for something without first putting it in you. When you understand this, you won't go through life thinking you're lacking, or that you don't measure up. You'll realize you've been preprogrammed for greatness. God has already deposited seeds of strength, wisdom, and creativity inside of you. All you have to do is trust Him, take the limits off, and step into who He created you to be.

This book is about helping you rediscover that version of yourself—the passionate, confident, victorious you. It's time to reignite your dreams, take back your joy, and embrace the abundant life God has already prepared for you.

—Joel Osteen

Contents

CHAPTER ONE
Rediscover the Forgotten You — 1

CHAPTER TWO
Believe In the True You — 25

CHAPTER THREE
Change Your Name — 47

CHAPTER FOUR
Build Yourself Up — 67

CHAPTER FIVE
Get Your Mind Going in the Right Direction — 89

CHAPTER SIX
Stand Strong as God's Masterpiece — 109

CHAPTER SEVEN
Know That You Are Destined for Greatness — 133

CHAPTER EIGHT
Forget the Past, Focus on the Future — 151

CHAPTER NINE
Declare Victory and Expect Favor — 169

CHAPTER TEN
Let Your Light Shine — 189

CHAPTER ONE

Rediscover the Forgotten You

Our God knows your disappointments, your mistakes, all that you've lost and hidden, and He is coming to restore the real you and love you back into wholeness.

Life has a way of changing us. At one time we were outgoing, excited about our dreams, grateful for our family. We saw the best in people, excelled at work, were positive and hopeful. Then life happens. We go through a disappointment and we lose a little joy. We make mistakes, and we lose a little sense of value. People do us wrong, and we lose a little passion. Our dream doesn't work out, and we lose a little confidence. One day, we look up and wonder where that other person went.

A man recently said to me, "Joel, I've lost myself. I used to be so passionate, so caring, but I don't know what happened. I don't even recognize who I am." He'd been through a loss. Things hadn't turned out the way he thought. Now he felt as though he was a fraction of the person he had been. But God didn't create you to start off excited about life, joyful, believing for your dreams, and then end up defeated, insecure, and lonely. That's life trying to change who you are.

You may have lost yourself, but the good news is you can find yourself. You can go back to who God made you to be. The real you is still there—the joyful you, the passionate you, the confident you, the

> *You may have lost yourself, but the good news is you can find yourself. You can go back to who God made you to be.*

victorious you. One reason Jesus came was to recover what was lost, to restore what was stolen, to heal what was broken, to give you beauty for ashes, joy for mourning. What you've lost is coming back. God is about to do a new thing. He's not going to leave you in a deficit. He sees what you've been through, and He's going to make up for it. He's going to breathe on you with new life, new passion, new opportunities, and new vision. You haven't seen the best version of you yet. It's still in front of you. But there's something you have to do. You can't sit on the sidelines feeling sorry for yourself, thinking you're washed up. *I've made so many mistakes. Why did those people do me wrong?* As long as you have a defeated mentality, you're going to get stuck where you are. You have to get back in the game. Stir up your faith. Start believing again. Start dreaming again. Start hoping again.

> *Start believing again. Start dreaming again. Start hoping again.*

WHERE ARE YOU?

In the book of Genesis, Adam and Eve were living in the magnificent Garden of Eden with its beautiful flowers, peaceful streams, and trees with luscious fruit. God would come in the cool of the day and talk with them. They were happy, confident, and secure. They would wake up excited about the new day, grateful for what God had given them, but then life happened. God told them to not eat the fruit from a certain tree, but the serpent deceived Eve, and she and Adam ate it. When they did, their consciences came to life, and they immediately felt guilty. They knew they had done wrong. They realized they were naked and were ashamed and embarrassed. So they ran and hid, sewing together some fig leaves to cover up. They got behind some trees to make sure they weren't visible.

> *"Adam, where is the real you? Where is the you I created?"*

When God came to visit them that evening, He called out, "Adam, where are you?" God wasn't asking this question to find an answer. He knew where they were. God was asking to get Adam to think, *Where are you?* Not just physically. He was asking

Adam about his state of mind, his attitude, how he saw himself. He was saying, "Adam, where is the real you? Where is the you I created? Where is the joyful you, the confident you, the valuable you, the peaceful you? Where has that person gone?" God is also asking us, "Where are you? Where is the you before you went through the disappointment, the you before the breakup, the you before the mistake, the you before the business slowed? Where is the passionate you, the friendly you, the kind you, the positive you, the hopeful you, the generous you who I created you to be?"

But too often, like Adam, because of mistakes and disappointments, we lose that person. We can look back and think, *I used to be so passionate about life. I used to have big dreams. I used to feel valuable and secure. I used to be outgoing and fun. I had a great personality. I don't know what happened to me.* You may have lost who you are, but God is going to bring that person back. Nothing that's happened to you has taken the real you.

> **Nothing that's happened to you has taken the real you.**

HIDING

Adam said to God, "When I heard Your voice, I was afraid, so I went and hid." How many of us are hiding? Because of things we've gone through, we're hiding our potential, hiding our personality, hiding our smile. We have so much to offer, but the way many people handle hurts, failures, and disappointments is to isolate. We disengage, turn off our feelings, push down any emotions, and don't pursue our dreams. We show up for work, but we're not really there. We have great ideas, but we don't share them. We're in the house physically with our family, but we've checked out emotionally. The pressure, the hurts, and the mistakes have caused us to go into a defense mode. We don't participate, don't answer the phone, don't interact with friends, and don't share our feelings. The enemy would love for you to live disengaged, unplugged, hiding your gifts, hiding your creativity, hiding your feelings. God is saying, "Where are you?

> *The enemy would love for you to live disengaged, unplugged, hiding your gifts, hiding your creativity, hiding your feelings.*

I created you to bloom, to blossom, to shine, to enjoy life, to be a blessing, to love, to laugh, to accomplish great things." But it will never happen if you're hiding behind mistakes, hiding behind hurts, hiding behind injustice.

"I wasn't treated right, Joel. That's why I'm bitter. I went through a breakup. They hurt me. That's why I'm not passionate anymore." "My spouse and I don't get along. She doesn't respect me. That's why I've checked out." The enemy is using these experiences to keep you in hiding, feeling ashamed, insecure, with no enthusiasm. But here's a key: God can't heal what's hidden. He's asking you to come out, to get engaged again, but He's not going to force you. You have to make the choice to come out of isolation, come out of fear, come out of shame, come out of regrets, and get back in the game.

> *God can't heal what's hidden.*

Can I encourage you to believe that the part of you that you lost is looking for you right now? The joy, the talent, the favor, the confidence—it's knocking on your door. The creative you, the outgoing you, the compassionate you, the generous you has been gone long enough. Now you have to do your part and get your fire back. Start taking some risks. "Well, if I get involved in another relationship, I may get hurt again. If I take this new opportunity, they may not treat me right or I may not be good at it." Yes, it's easier to stay in hiding. If you unplug, if you disengage, you might not experience as much hurt, pain, or disappointment. But you'll also never experience the joy, the love, the favor, and the victory that makes life so rewarding and fulfilling. The enemy doesn't want you engaged, motivated, passionate, feeling good about anything. He'd love for you to go through life feeling numb, isolated, never showing this world who God made you to be. Don't fall into that trap. You may get knocked down, but don't go into hiding. That disappointment is not final. Get back up again. You made a mistake. Don't beat yourself up and live in regret for five years. Ask for forgiveness and move forward. God doesn't remember your sins and mistakes, so why are you remembering them? Those are forces trying to get you to unplug, to disengage, so you don't fulfill your purpose.

> *You may get knocked down, but don't go into hiding.*

WHAT LIES ARE YOU BELIEVING?

> *Failure is an event, not a person. You don't have to go into hiding.*

Maybe your dream didn't work out. You put a lot of effort into the business, but it failed. Failure is an event, not a person. You don't have to go into hiding. That's not who you are. You're not a failure. You're a child of the Most High God. Any person who's ever done anything significant has had some failures, disappointments, and setbacks. That's not the time to disengage and give up on your dreams. If it didn't happen your way, that means God has something better coming.

Or perhaps people have hurt you. They put you at a disadvantage. Thoughts will try to convince you that you're lacking, you're not up to par. *If you were more attractive, if you were more talented, if you had a better personality, this wouldn't have happened.* It's easy to go into hiding, to live insecure, feeling not valuable. Don't believe those lies. You're made in the image of Almighty God. People can't make

> *People can't make you feel inferior unless you give them permission.*

you feel inferior unless you give them permission. They don't determine your worth and value. What they say about you or how they treat you doesn't change who God made you to be. Quit giving them permission.

When I was in junior high, I was very outgoing and had a lot of friends. We played sports together. I was confident, secure, always making people laugh. But when I got into high school, all my friends kept growing taller, but I didn't. I went into my freshman year at four feet nine inches tall. People called me "Peanut." The thoughts started coming: *You're too short. You're at a disadvantage. People are making fun of you.* I let that insecurity in, and it started to affect my confidence. Soon I wasn't as outgoing. I started to hide my personality, becoming quieter and more reserved. I tried out for the baseball team. In Little League, I had always been one of the best players, on the all-star team every year. But now in high school, the other players were so much bigger and stronger. We were all in the gym, waiting to see who made the team. The coach called out the names one by one. One friend made it, then another and another and another. They all made the team. I waited and waited, thinking surely my name was next, but I didn't make it. The coach called me in afterward and said, "Joel, you're a good player, but you're just too small to play at this level."

That was the last thing I needed to hear. For years I let that affect my self-image, my confidence, my personality. I dealt with it the way many of us do: I went into hiding. I wasn't as outgoing. When certain opportunities came, I would shrink back, unsure of myself, wondering what people would think. *Maybe I'm not talented enough.* But down in my spirit I could hear God whispering, "Joel, where are you? Where is that person who I created, so strong, confident, fun, outgoing? Why are you shrinking back, letting someone else determine your value, when you have so much more to offer?" I had to make the decision to come out of hiding, to not worry about what other people think, to not let disappointments take my passion. If I had not done that, I wouldn't be where I am today. Is there some area where you need to come out of hiding? You've let what didn't work out, what someone said, or how you were raised cause you to shrink back, to unplug, and now we're not seeing the best of you.

> *Is there some area where you need to come out of hiding?*

When Adam made that mistake, he went into hiding. He tried to check out, but notice how God came looking for him. God could have said, "Too bad, Adam. You blew it. You had your chance." But God never gives up on us, even when we hide, even when we lose the person He made us to be. He keeps coming after us, saying, "Where are you? I miss you. I need you. I can restore you." As I did, maybe you've let a disappointment or a mistake cause you to hide your personality, hide your smile, hide your passion. You used to have big dreams, you used to fight for your family, you used to be passionate about your walk with God, but you've disengaged, you've checked out, thinking it's not worth it. Can I tell you that God is looking for you—not the partial you, not the shrunk back version, not the intimidated you? Where is the confident you, where is the outgoing you, where is the talented you? Where is that you before the coach told you that you're too small? Where is the you before you ate the forbidden fruit? That's who God is looking for—the true you, not the watered down you.

> *Where is the confident you, where is the outgoing you, where is the talented you?*

The you who dreamed big, the you who knew all things are possible. The you who took steps of faith, the you who was determined to set new standards. The you who didn't let doubt and fear and negativity talk you out of your goals. That's who God is looking for. I believe that part of you that you lost is coming back today. God is restoring dreams, restoring passion, restoring confidence, restoring value, restoring vision, creativity, talent, goals, and joy. This is a new day. The full you is coming back.

WHO TOLD YOU THAT?

Adam told God he was hiding because he was naked. He felt ashamed and embarrassed. The second question God asked was, "Adam, who told you that you were naked?" Again, God wasn't asking to get the information. He wanted Adam to realize where that thought came from, that it was the enemy deceiving him. It's no different today. The enemy will whisper his lies, trying to deceive you into hiding. "You're not talented enough. You've made too many mistakes. You'll never be successful. You come from the wrong family." You need to ask yourself where the negative thoughts are coming from. If they're discouraging you, pushing you down, making you feel unworthy, you can be certain they are not from God. Don't give them the time of day. Let them go in one ear and out the other.

When I didn't make the baseball team, the coach was just doing his job, judging by the physical. But people don't determine our value. I could hear God saying, "Joel, who told you you're too small? Who told you that you're not up to par? I created you in My own image. You are fearfully and wonderfully made. I call you a masterpiece. I put a crown of favor on your head."

You need to listen to what God says about you and not all the negative chatter. You may have made poor choices and gotten off course. Who told you that mistake stopped your purpose? Who told you that you're washed up, unworthy, made to sit on the sidelines? That's the accuser trying to keep you in hiding, feeling guilty, not good enough, so you won't pursue your dreams, you won't accomplish your

> *You need to listen to what God says about you and not all the negative chatter.*

assignment. Don't believe those lies. God's mercy is bigger than any mistake you've made. He already took into account every failure, every wrong turn, every compromise. He has mercy, restoration, and new beginnings already lined up. His calling on your life is irrevocable. He doesn't change His mind. What He started He will finish, but you have to do your part and come out of hiding. Come out of shame. Come out of guilt. Get back in the game. Your family needs you fully engaged. Your children need you healthy and whole. Your friends need you—not the partial you, but the full you, the outgoing you, the loving you, the friendly you.

Maybe you went through a breakup and had a divorce. Who told you that you'll never be happy again? Who told you that disappointment has ruined your future, that you'll never meet anyone?

The enemy wouldn't be telling you those lies if there wasn't something awesome in your future.

That's why he's trying to deceive you into living negative, doubting, thinking you've missed your chance. Tune that out. God has beauty for the ashes. The right person, a divine connection, is already en route. Your latter days will be better than your former days. Who told you that you're not talented enough? Who told you that all you can make in school are C's and not A's? Who told you that you'll never be successful, that you're limited by your family, your background, your education? That's the enemy doing what he did in the Garden of Eden, trying to deceive you into hiding your gifts, hiding your talents. Don't believe his lies. God has put greatness in you. There are ideas, creativity, and businesses in you. He created you to bloom, to blossom, to go where no one in your family has gone. That's why the enemy fights so hard to try to keep you pushed down, feeling inadequate, where you have a limited vision. No, come out of hiding. God is about to enlarge your territory. He's about to expand your influence, increase your resources. You haven't seen, heard, or imagined what He has in store. He's just waiting for you to come back to who you are—the bold you, the confident you, the faith-filled you, the dreaming you, the mighty hero you.

> *He's just waiting for you to come back to who you are—the bold you, the confident you, the faith-filled you, the dreaming you, the mighty hero you.*

WHEN YOU COME OUT OF HIDING

I saw a video about a stray dog that was about a year old. He lived behind a big dumpster in an alley in a busy downtown area. One cold, rainy night, a couple was throwing away some trash and noticed the dog shriveled up in the corner, shaking, so frail and thin. He had lost most of his hair. The young woman felt sorry and went over to help it, but the dog got defensive, growled and showed his teeth and kept his paws out. But the woman wouldn't give up. She went home and got some food and a blanket. This time she got down on her knees to be more at the dog's level. She put some food out and spoke softly and gently. Little by little, the dog began to let down his defenses. She was able to get close enough to pet the dog. After about an hour, she gained the dog's trust enough and was able to pick it up. She and her husband took it home, not knowing if the dog would live. In her house, the dog went to a corner and would never lift his head, so afraid and insecure. But the woman just kept loving it, feeding it, doing her best to win it over. Then the video fast-forwarded one year. You wouldn't believe it was the same dog. This dog was so playful and happy, jumping up on them, spinning around in circles, fetching things in the backyard.

That playful, healthy, loving dog was in there the whole time. But when you go through hurts, mistreatment, and bad breaks, there's a natural tendency to isolate, disengage, and become angry. We put up defenses and think, *This is just who I am. I'm bitter about my bad childhood. I'm angry because my company did me wrong. I've given up on my dreams because I made poor choices. Look at where I am.* Like that little dog, there is so much more in you. You're just letting that defense mechanism cause you to isolate and push others away, thinking that staying in hiding is the way to deal with it. But that is not a good option. God has seen everything you've been through—who hurt you, who didn't keep their word, the mistakes you've made, the times you took the wrong turn. Now you're in the corner, not wanting anyone to help. Like the young woman who went with compassion and rescued the dog, God is coming to you. He's calling your name. If you come out of hiding, if you let down your defenses and give it another chance, you'll discover a life greater than

> *When you go through hurts, mistreatment, and bad breaks, there's a natural tendency to isolate, disengage, and become angry.*

you ever dreamed. God is not finished with you. He didn't create you and then decide to walk away because of mistakes, or neglect, or bad breaks. He's a God who restores, a God who has new beginnings. Today He's saying, "Where are you? Let Me turn things around. Let Me love you back into wholeness. Let Me pay you back for the unfair things."

It's not always something big. It may be just hiding a part of your personality, letting insecurity creep in or what other people think hold you back and keep you from blossoming into who you were created to be. It may be letting mistakes convince you to feel unworthy. You know you have so much more in you. You can feel God calling you to step up, to get out of your comfort zone, but it's much easier to stay in hiding, not having to stretch. Yes, it's easier, but you'll never be fulfilled if you settle for less than what God put in you. There will always be a subtle unrest, a slight uneasiness. That's God saying, "Step into My purpose for your life."

> *You'll never be fulfilled if you settle for less than what God put in you.*

WHAT IS THE STILL SMALL VOICE SAYING?

In 1 Kings 18, the prophet Elijah had just called down fire from heaven and destroyed 450 false prophets. He had just prayed for rain and saw a three-and-a-half-year drought come to an end. He had just outrun a chariot for twenty miles. He was so powerful and anointed that you would never think he had a down moment. But soon after all that success he was so depressed he wanted to die. When King Ahab's wife heard about the prophets he destroyed, she sent word, saying, "I'm going to kill you by this time tomorrow." Elijah got so afraid, so panicked, that he took off running for his life into the wilderness. You can be devoted, faithful, anointed, and still have times when you lose who you are. Elijah ended up hiding in a cave. He went into isolation, didn't want to talk to anyone. His attitude was: *I'm done. This is the end of my life.* But God came to him in the cave and said, "Elijah, what are you doing here?" He was saying, "This is not who I

> *You can be devoted, faithful, anointed, and still have times when you lose who you are.*

made you to be, afraid, intimidated, defeated. You've lost who you are: bold, confident, faith filled." Elijah answered, "God, these people are after me, and I'm the only one serving You. Everyone else turned away."

God told Elijah to go and stand outside the cave. After a mighty wind, an earthquake, and a fire, God spoke to him again in a still small voice. I can imagine Elijah leaning in, listening so intently. *What is God going to tell me this time?* God said again, "What are you doing here?" As powerful as Elijah was, he'd lost a part of himself. He got distracted and forgot who he was. God didn't say, "Elijah, I feel sorry for you. I know it's been rough. Just settle here in the cave." No, God said, "Elijah, go back the way you came." God was saying, "Come out of hiding and go back to who I say you are—powerful, anointed, favored, victorious."

Maybe today, like Elijah, you're committed, you're faithful, and you're blessed, but you've lost part of yourself. Things have happened that have taken your joy, limited your vision, stopped your creativity. Now you've settled in that area, not pursuing your dreams, not enjoying your family, not passionate about life. God is saying, "Come out of hiding and go back to who I created you to be." Get your fire back. Get your dream back. No more isolating, checking out, being there but not engaging. I know things happen that are not fair, things you don't understand, but God sees it. That's not how your story ends. This is a new day. I believe and declare that part of you that you lost is coming back. The confident you, the joyful you, the passionate you, the valuable you, the successful you is coming back.

CHAPTER TWO

Believe In the True You

Despite our flaws and weaknesses, the beauty of our God is that He specializes in removing everything that's not the true you, the one who He created, and He will keep working until the best you comes out.

Inside of every one of us is a blessed person, someone who is confident, valuable, and talented. The Scripture says, "You have been fearfully and wonderfully made." The word *fearful* in the original language means "to stand in awe, to reverence." It implies honor and respect. When God created you, He stood back in reverence. He looked at you in awe. God didn't make anyone average. He didn't say, "I didn't do very good on that one. They have a bunch of flaws. They're going to be angry, insecure, and jealous." You've been exceptionally made. But as we go through life, we make mistakes, develop bad habits, and people do us wrong. Shame comes, guilt comes, insecurity comes. We don't feel valued. We feel condemned. *How can I be successful? Look what I've been through. I'm struggling with an addiction. I'm not that talented.* But underneath the insecurity, the bad breaks, and the failures, there's the true you, the one who God created.

> **Underneath the insecurity, the bad breaks, and the failures, there's the true you, the one who God created.**

The blessed you, the happy you, the successful you, the forgiven you. It's still in you.

The beauty of our God is, He always remembers the true you. He still remembers the reverence He felt when He created you. Despite all our flaws, weaknesses, and disappointments, He still sees the masterpiece. He still knows who you really are.

Life tries to put all these things on you—impatience, jealousy, bad breaks—to keep the true you from coming out. The good news is, God is not going to leave us like that. He's going to keep working on us, making us, molding us, until the true you comes out, the free you, the blessed you, the patient you, the victorious you. God specializes in removing everything that's not the true you.

"Joel, I'll always struggle with this addiction. I've had it since high school. It's just who I am." No, that is not who you are. That's something the enemy put on you to try to keep the true you from ever coming out. The true you is free. The true you is whole. That addiction is not how your story ends. God is working right now. You may have gone through bad breaks, someone walked out on you, or you weren't raised in a good environment. It's easy to carry the hurts and let them limit your vision. It's easy to carry the shame, to go around feeling unworthy, like you don't deserve to be blessed. Do not believe those lies. The enemy would love for you to live discouraged, thinking nothing good is in your future. No, the true you is still in you. That's the happy you, the restored you, the valuable you. What people did to you didn't stop the true you. What wasn't fair didn't change who God created you to be. He's in the process right now of removing everything that's not the true you. The angry you is not the true you. You may think, *I'm just hot-tempered. I can't help it. My father was this way, and so was my grandfather.* That's not who you really are. It may be the way you are now, but you're the one to break the cycle. You're the one to see it come to an end. The true you is calm, cool, and collected. Don't buy into the lies that you can't change. God is removing everything that's not the true you. He loves you too much to leave you alone. He's going to keep working on you until He sees the masterpiece He created you to be.

> *The true you is still in you.*

> *The true you is calm, cool, and collected. Don't buy into the lies that you can't change.*

THE REMOVAL OF WHAT'S NOT YOU

In the early 1500s, a twenty-six-year-old artist named Michelangelo had a dream to sculpt King David out of a huge piece of marble, a twelve-thousand-pound block, that stood over twenty feet tall. He worked tirelessly for three years, chiseling and shaping with great precision and great detail. When he revealed the finished product, this seventeen-foot-tall marble image of David, it was magnificent, so beautiful, so inspiring. Someone asked Michelangelo how he could accomplish such an incredible feat, how could he make this amazing statue out of a piece of marble. He said, "I had a vision in my mind of King David, and I just kept removing everything that wasn't him."

That's the way God is. He knows who we really are. He can see the masterpiece in the rock. Throughout our lives, He'll keep removing things that are not who we are—the impatience, the insecurity, the unworthiness. "I'm not valuable. Look at what I've been through." Chisel, chisel. That's not who you are. There's the pride, the arrogance. Chisel, chisel. That doesn't belong on you. "They hurt me. They did me wrong." Chisel, chisel. The unforgiveness and resentment has to come off. "I'll never do something great. Nobody in my family is successful. I'm not that talented." Chisel, chisel. That limited mindset, that mediocrity, doesn't belong on you. It may try to come, try to distort your image, try to affect your personality, try to limit your future. The good news is, we have someone far greater than Michelangelo working on us. We have the Creator of the universe, the God who makes spectacular solar systems, magnificent mountain ranges, and amazing sunsets. He's the artist who's working on you. He's chiseling away everything that's not the true you.

He can see things that we can't see. So often we let our circumstances determine who we are. We let how people treat us determine our value. We let how good we perform determine our worth. God looks beyond all that. In the Scripture, He sees the giant killer in the shepherd boy David. He sees a mighty hero in Gideon, who's hiding in a winepress, afraid and intimidated by his enemies. He

> *We let our circumstances determine who we are. We let how people treat us determine our value. We let how good we perform determine our worth.*

sees a respectful, honored woman in a former prostitute named Rahab who is included in the family line of Jesus. God knows what's in you. You may have made mistakes, done things you're not proud of. God sees the redeemed you, the restored you, the honored you. You may be intimidated, thinking you're not that talented. God sees the giant killer. He sees the history maker in you. Maybe life has thrown you curves; you've been hurt, abandoned, or betrayed. God sees the valuable you, the blessed you, the favored you. Nothing that's happened has changed the true you. God looks beyond our mistakes, the hurts, the bad breaks, and He sees who He created you to be. He hasn't lost the vision of who you are. The good news is, God still has the chisel. He still knows what to remove so the best you will come out—the talented you, the confident you, the loving you, the free you.

DON'T FIGHT THE CHISEL

Sometimes when God chisels, it's uncomfortable. We don't like it. "I don't want to bite my tongue. I don't want to overlook the offense. I want to tell them off." Be pliable. Work with God. Let Him remove the hardness that's keeping you from going to new levels. Driving to work, you get caught in traffic construction on the freeway. Some jerk—I mean some person—cuts you off. You'll be tempted to get upset and let it sour your day. Recognize what's happening. God is chiseling away the impatience. He's giving you an opportunity to grow. The impatient you will try to keep the true you from coming out. At the office, coworkers are taking your ideas, and you're not getting the credit you deserve. You could live offended and try to get revenge, pay them back. No, let God be your vindicator. Let Him fight your battles. He sees what's happening. He knows what's not fair. He has the chisel out. You think it's about them, but really, it's about you. That's an opportunity to show God that you trust Him, that you'll stay in peace and not let people steal your joy.

Sometimes God will remove things we don't understand. He'll remove a friend who's pulling us down, causing us to compromise. We don't like the change. We were comfortable. Now we're going to have to stretch and grow.

> *God knows what He's doing. He's not going to leave something on you that will keep you from your purpose.*

Don't fight the chisel. God knows what He's doing. He's not going to leave something on you that will keep you from your purpose. He'll never ask you to do something and then not give you the ability to do it. If He's asking you to walk away, you know a season is coming to an end. That's the chisel at work. If you're stubborn, if you fight it, you're going to miss the greater things God has in store. He's not trying to take something from you; He's trying to get something better to you. He wants to bring out the true you. The more blessed, more successful, more peaceful you.

A friend of mine worked for the same company for over twenty years. He's the nicest person in the world, always kind, respectful, going the extra mile. He called one day and said, "Joel, I just got fired from my job. They said I didn't have a good attitude, so they were letting me go." I almost fell out of my chair. This would be like Mother Theresa getting fired. I couldn't believe it. But sometimes God will close a door because we're stagnant. If He didn't push us into our destiny, the true us would never come out. We don't realize that there's so much more in us, the gifts, talents, potential. God will chisel away things that are keeping you from your greatness. Sometimes they're good things, but they're not the best. Trust Him when you don't understand. He won't remove something unless He has something better coming. He won't use the chisel if it's not going to make you better. It may hurt at the time, it may be uncomfortable, but God knows what He's doing. About six months later, my friend called and was so excited. He'd just gotten his dream job of running a large company. He said, "I never knew this was in me. I never imagined I would be this successful, this fulfilled."

> *He won't remove something unless He has something better coming.*

Let God remove what He knows is keeping you from the true you. Unforgiveness will keep you from shining. Insecurity, compromise, and anger will block the best you from coming out. Be willing to change. We don't have to be perfect, but we should be growing. We should be better now than we were five years ago. We should be kinder, more respectful, have a better attitude. We should be more confident, more secure. We should forgive more quickly, overlook offenses more easily.

> *We don't have to be perfect, but we should be growing.*

We should compromise less and resist temptation more often. That means we're letting the chisel chip away things that are hindering our growth. We're seeing more of the true you coming out. Stay focused; don't give up hope on finding the forgotten you—the person full of potential and promise that you were created to be.

LOOK BEYOND THE IMPERFECTIONS

Fifty years before Michelangelo carved the statue of David out of that large block of marble, two of the most accomplished sculptors of that time looked at the slab and said there was no way they could work with it. It had too many flaws, too many imperfections. They were given the chance first, but they turned it down because the marble had too many blemishes, too many defects. Decades later, young Michelangelo came along. He saw the same block of marble, the same defects, the same flaws, but he looked beyond the imperfections. He said, "I see a masterpiece in this stone. I see King David in this slab."

Like those first two artists, other people may look

at you and think, *They'll never amount to much. Look at their failures, their weaknesses. They struggle with an addiction. Look at what they've been through, all the bad breaks, the disappointments.* All they see is your flaws, your blemishes, what hasn't worked out. They may discount you and write you off. Then like Michelangelo did, God comes along. He says, "Hey, wait a minute. Don't abandon that piece of marble. Yes, I see flaws. I see weaknesses, but I see something else. I see a blessed, strong, forgiven, favored child of the Most High God." It's not that God doesn't see the flaws, but He knows how to remove the flaws. He knows how to make you and mold you to where the best you comes out.

> *It's not that God doesn't see the flaws, but He knows how to remove the flaws.*

FROM SHIFTING SAND TO A ROCK

This is what happened with Peter. In Luke 5, Jesus was standing on the shore of the Sea of Galilee teaching the people, but they were crowding around Him. He saw Peter washing his nets and asked if He could borrow his boat to put out a little from the shore and teach out of the boat. Peter agreed, and when Jesus finished teaching, He told Peter to put out into deep water and let down his nets. When he did, he caught so many fish that his nets began to break, and it took a second boat to hold all the fish. Astonished, Peter fell on his knees and said, "Please, Lord, leave me. I'm too much of a sinner to be around You." Peter was a rough fisherman, known for cursing, being hot-tempered, having flaws and weaknesses. Yet God chose him to be His disciple, one of the twelve who would change the world. Out of all the people Jesus could have chosen, He didn't choose a religious leader from the temple, a priest from a synagogue, or a mayor of a city. He chose Peter.

Jesus already knew that Peter would deny Him three times. He already knew Peter was hot-tempered, that he would curse. He already knew Peter would fall asleep in the Garden of Gethsemane when He needed him the most, then he would try to defend Jesus and pull out his sword and cut off the ear of a servant of the high priest. Why would Jesus choose someone like Peter? Because God looks beyond the flaws, the mistakes, the weaknesses, and He sees what we can become. He hasn't lost the vision of the true you, how He made you before you were formed in your mother's womb. Jesus looked at Peter and said, "You are Simon, but you shall be called Peter." The name Simon represents shifting sand, being unstable, inconsistent, but Peter means rock. Jesus was telling him who the true you was. At one point, Jesus said, "You are Peter, and upon this rock I will build my church." When Jesus said that, Peter was anything but a rock. He was unreliable, the one who called himself a sinful man. Yet God called out the true Peter, the faithful Peter. It didn't happen overnight, but God kept chiseling away Peter's weaknesses, chiseling away the hot temper, chiseling away the inconsistencies.

When the church was starting in the book of Acts, who gave the inaugural address on the day of Pentecost? Peter had this prominent position. But now it wasn't the impulsive Peter, the inconsistent Peter, the deny-Jesus Peter. This was the rock. It was the true Peter, the faithful Peter, the strong Peter, the anointed Peter, the powerful Peter. Here's what I'm saying: Don't get discouraged because of who you are right now. God still has His chisel. He's still removing things that are limiting your destiny. You haven't seen your best days. The rock in you is still going to come out. That's the successful you, the holy you, the favored you.

DON'T GET TALKED OUT OF IT

> *There will always be people who try to discount you, tell you what you can't become, how you're not talented enough, you've made too many mistakes. Don't let them talk you out of becoming the true you.*

Like those two artists who saw the slab of marble but said it had too many flaws, there will always be people who try to discount you, tell you what you can't become, how you're not talented enough, you've made too many mistakes. Don't let them talk you out of becoming the true you. The good news is, they're not your artist. They don't have the chisel. You're not dependent on what they think or what they can do. Your sculptor is the Most High God. He has not lost the vision of who He created you to be.

My dad was raised very poor. His family were cotton farmers who lost everything in the Great Depression. His mother made ten cents an hour washing people's clothes. There were times when they didn't have enough money for food. He went to school with holes in his pants and his shoes, and eventually he had to drop out of high school to work on the farm. At seventeen years old, he gave his life to Christ, the first one in his family. He felt the calling to become a minister, but he had no money, a poor education, and no training. But he told his parents he was going to leave the farm and go out and start ministering. They said, "John, you don't know how to minister. You're going to get out there and fail. You better stay on the farm and work with us." They loved their son, but they could only see the limited John, the poor John, the not-talented John, the defeated John. They looked at that marble, so to speak, and said, "Nothing good can come out of that. Look at all the flaws, the deficiencies, the imperfections." If Daddy had believed who they said he was, he would never have fulfilled his destiny. People can't see what God put in you. Don't let their negative words limit your life. Tune it out. You're not who people say you are; you are who God says you are.. He says you have greatness in you. He says you are destined to leave your mark.

My father grew up with this limited mindset, this poverty mentality. All he had known was struggle, lack, and mediocrity. But we serve a God who has a chisel. He doesn't let how you were raised, what you didn't get, or the odds being against you keep you from your purpose. Little by little, God removed the poverty mindset. He chiseled away the mediocrity, the "not good enough." Against all odds, my father rose up and did great things. He pastored churches, founded Lakewood, and impacted the world. In that penniless, disadvantaged, poorly educated seventeen-year-old man was a world changer, a history maker. If you only knew what was in you. The true you is not limited by your environment. You are not dependent on what other people think about you. The true you is not at a disadvantage because you have flaws and weaknesses.

> *If you only knew what was in you.*

The enemy would love for us to go through life feeling inferior, focused on our weaknesses, weighed down with regrets, guilty from past mistakes, condemned, ashamed. But what the enemy put on you, God is about to take off you. This is a new day. The chisel is at

> *He's chiseling away wrong mindsets, chiseling away negative words that have been spoken, chiseling away guilt and shame, chiseling away hurts, brokenness, offenses.*

work. He's chiseling away wrong mindsets, chiseling away negative words that have been spoken, chiseling away guilt and shame, chiseling away hurts, brokenness, offenses. You're about to step into a new level of your destiny—the blessed you, the free you, the healthiest you, the victorious you.

A TROPHY OF HIS GRACE

I know a young woman who was raised in a very dysfunctional home. When she was seven years old, the police showed up at her house and told her to put her belongings in a trash bag, that she was going to spend the night somewhere else. She grabbed her pajamas and toothbrush and was taken to a shelter. Her mother and stepfather were arrested for child abuse. She had never met her biological father, but eventually she was turned over to him, which wasn't any better. He was on drugs, in and out of jail. She couldn't understand why no one would love her and became very angry. She got to the point where she built up walls so she didn't have to feel. She became numb to the pain. She didn't feel happy, sad, or depressed. She felt nothing. When she was sixteen, she moved out on her own, hurting, broken, and lonely. By the grace of God, she showed up at Lakewood and heard us talking about how God is our Heavenly Father, how He has good things in store for us, how He will give beauty for the ashes. She had never felt that love before. She had never had anyone speak faith and victory into her and tell her who she really was. One day, she gave her life to Christ. She said, "I realized I was no longer an orphan. I was adopted by my Heavenly Father." The right people began to show up, doors began to open. Today that beautiful young woman, Desiree, is on staff with us at Lakewood. She has the joy, the smile, the victory. Here's what I've learned: God will not leave you at a deficit. What you didn't get, what wasn't fair, what you feel robbed of, God is going to make it up to you. He's going to pay you back for the unfair things.

> *God will not leave you at a deficit. What you didn't get, what wasn't fair, what you feel robbed of, God is going to make it up to you.*

If you had seen Desiree years back, you would have seen the broken you, the abandoned you, the angry you. All these things the enemy had put on her to try to keep her from her destiny. But underneath the shame, the anger, and the rejection was the masterpiece. There was this beautiful, confident, radiant, talented young woman.

The three years that Michelangelo worked on sculpting David, he did it all in private. He wouldn't let anyone come in. When he finished, he revealed it to the public. Now five hundred million people have seen it in person. You think about that old slab of rock, with flaws and weaknesses that other artists rejected, yet it's been seen by a half billion people. When God is working on you, chiseling away what's not necessary, He'll often do it in private. He'll keep you hidden, unnoticed. But when it's your time, when God says you're ready, He'll cause you to be seen. You'll become a trophy of His grace, where people think, *Wasn't that the old rock that had flaws? Wasn't that the fisherman, and now he's up there leading? Isn't that the young boy from the Great Depression, and now he's the pastor? Wasn't she abandoned by her parents, and look at her now?* God is going to cause you to shine, to be an example of what He can do despite imperfections, despite what life throws your way.

> **When it's your time, when God says you're ready, He'll cause you to be seen.**

You may have some things that are limiting you now, but don't worry, God still has His chisel. He's still working on you. The true you is about to come out. What's holding you back is being broken, the shame is being removed. You're about to step into favor, freedom, and wholeness and become the exceptional and wonderful person you were designed to be.

CHAPTER THREE

Change Your Name

People and circumstances may have named you something negative, something you're not, but your Heavenly Father is the only One who has the right to name you, and His name overrides all others.

It's easy to go through life letting people and circumstances put names on us, such as average, unqualified, addicted, poor. Sometimes our own thoughts have named us unattractive, not talented, not good enough, unworthy. As long as you're wearing these names, believing the lies that people and circumstances have told you, it's going to keep you from your potential. Who do you believe you are? How do you see yourself? God named you blessed, prosperous, talented, victorious, one of a kind. People will call you ordinary, average, nothing special. If you accept those names, you'll become ordinary, average, nothing special. What's holding many people back is they have the wrong name.

A man was walking down a busy street in Thailand. He came upon a tattoo shop. In the window he saw samples of many of the tattoos they offered. One said, "Born to Lose." He couldn't believe anyone would have that tattooed on their body. The owner came

> *Is your name "Born to Lose" or "Born to Win"?*

out and they struck up a conversation. He asked the owner if anyone ever got the "Born to Lose" tattoo. The Thai owner nodded his head yes and said, "Before tattooed on body, tattooed on mind." He's exactly right. If you accept the name in your mind, if you believe the negative things people say about you, if you let circumstances name you, you're giving it the right to come to pass. Is your name "Born to Lose" or "Born to Win"? Is your name poor, broke, in debt, or is your name prosperous, blessed, more than enough? Is your name sick, tired, can't get well, or is your name healthy, whole, energetic? Have you let life name you addicted, limited, always struggling, or do you go by what God named you: free, victorious, overcomer, well able? You need to change any name that's telling you something negative. Hold on to this truth: You are blessed—right now, as a beloved child of God. As you press forward, reclaiming your passion, reigniting your dreams, and stepping into the life you were born to live, you're not doing it alone. God's favor is going before you, working behind the scenes to restore every good thing meant for you.

WHAT GOD NAMES YOU OVERRIDES ALL NAMES

In the Scripture, Jacob's wife Rachel died after giving birth to her second child. The baby was born fine, but she was in so much pain, so much distress. Just before she died, she named the baby Ben-Oni, which means "son of my sorrow." Although the baby boy didn't do anything wrong, he was going to have to go through life being called "son of sorrow." Back in those days, the names given to children were very significant. They would set the direction for their lives. Today we name our children what we think sounds good, names that are popular, but back then the name could help determine their destiny. It looked as though little Ben-Oni was just in bad luck. His mother was in pain, and she took out her misery on him. She had pronounced that he would live a sorrowful, painful, depressing life.

Sometimes the people who should have been speaking faith over you—affirming you, naming you victorious, talented, a treasure—have done just the opposite. Because they're in pain, have issues, and are hurting, they've named you failure, not good enough. They may not say it, but they make you feel that way. They're always putting you down, never encouraging, never showing love and affection. The good news is, people don't have the final say. Your parents, those who have raised you, may not have named you what they should have. You could easily go by the name inferior, not talented, nothing special, but God has the final say. What He names you overrides what people name you. They may name you son of sorrow, son of pain, son of misery, but God names you son of victory, son of favor, son of blessing. Don't let negative words people have spoken over you, how you were raised, what you didn't get, determine your destiny. Change your name.

> *Sometimes the people who should have been speaking faith over you—affirming you, naming you victorious, talented, a treasure—have done just the opposite.*

A few minutes after Rachel died, Jacob came running in. The nurses handed him the baby and said, "Here's your son. Rachel named him Ben-Oni." When Jacob heard that name, something rose up inside. He said, "No, that is not his name. No matter what's happened in the past, no matter what somebody else said, his name will not be son of sorrow. His name will be Benjamin," which means "son of strength, son of power." In one moment, with that one name change, he went from son of sorrow to son of strength. Benjamin grew up to be a great leader. Out of his genes, out of his family line, came King Saul, the first king of Israel. God had a great destiny for Benjamin, an assignment, but He knew that if he'd gone around being called son of sorrow, son of misery, that would have gotten inside. He would have seen himself as limited and defeated, so both his earthly father and his Heavenly Father stepped in and said, "No, he's not a son of sorrow, he's not a son of disappointment, he's not a son of defeat. This child is a son of destiny. This child has greatness in him. This child is a son of strength."

Maybe someone has tried to name you average, not talented, unattractive, too many mistakes. God is saying to you what Jacob said to Benjamin, "I'm changing your name. No more son of sorrow, son of not good enough, son of broken dreams, son of disappointment. I'm renaming you son of strength, daughter of destiny, child of influence, child of greatness." Now you have to do your part and get rid of all the old names.

DON'T LET THE NEGATIVE NAME GET INSIDE

> *You are not who people call you; you are what you answer to.*

You can't stop people from saying negative things. But I've learned that you are not who people call you; you are what you answer to. They may call you slow, average, washed up, clumsy. That's okay, just don't answer to it. When thoughts say, *Hello, fearful, depressed, inferior*, don't give them the time of day. Just respond, "You must not be talking to me. That's not who I am. I am confident. I am secure. I am talented. I am victorious." *Hello, sick, tired, limited, chronic pain.* "Sorry, there's no one here by that name. You must have the wrong address. I am healthy, whole, strong. That's who lives here." *Hello, poor, broke, in debt, can't get ahead.* "Sorry, no one by that name is home." When you hear blessed, prosperous, more than enough, lend and not borrow, that's when you need to pay attention.

> *Are you answering to something that you're not?*

Are you answering to something that you're not?

Quit giving your time and energy to letting those negative thoughts play. That's not who you are. When voices whisper that you're washed up, guilty, unworthy, a failure, recognize what's happening. They're trying to rename you. When you hear forgiven, redeemed, restored, that's when you need to listen. *Hello, unqualified, inexperienced, less-than.* "Excuse me, did you mean anointed, highly favored, well able? That's who I am." When thoughts tell you, *You're unattractive. You don't have a good personality. You're too short. Nobody wants to be around you*, don't give that the time of day. When you hear, *Hello, good looking, sharp, attractive, fun, well off*, you want to say, "Yes, what can I do for you? Now you're calling my name." Answer to victorious, answer to more than a conqueror, answer to fearfully and wonderfully made.

People may call you many things, but you don't have to let it get in you. Go back to who God says you are. Let your Heavenly Father name you, not people, not mistakes, not your past. He calls you exceptional. He calls you redeemed and forgiven. He calls you healthy and free.

> **People may call you many things, but you don't have to let it get in you.**

He calls you one of a kind, a history maker, a giant killer. He calls you a son of strength, a daughter of destiny. Your part is to let what He names you override all the other names. Your assignment is too important to go through life wearing the names inferior, washed up, not talented, not attractive, average. I'm asking you to change your name, not on your driver's license but in your mind. Get in agreement with God.

REMEMBER WHAT YOUR REAL NAME MEANS

A friend of mine grew up in El Salvador. His father was an alcoholic and would become very violent when he was drinking. After his father left the family when he was a small child, his mother came to the United States, and he was raised by his grandparents. When he was a young boy, he felt lost. He did very poorly in school, didn't interact socially with people. He had nightmares that terrified him. One day he overheard his grandparents talking about how he was mentally impaired, how he was a slow learner and needed help. They sent him to a psychiatrist who confirmed that he had learning disabilities.

Over the years, he was told again and again that he would never amount to much. He wasn't smart enough, not good enough, not talented enough.

At ten years old, this boy was about to move to the States with his mother. He told his grandfather that he needed an American name. He had never heard his grandfather say one thing positive about him. He never encouraged him or spoke faith into him. But his grandfather started thinking intently and finally said, "Okay, son, this name needs to be something strong, something that says courage, valor, exceptional. It needs to be the name of a great leader, a genius, someone who will impact the world." He paused for a bit, then said, "I've got it. Your name will be Erwin." This boy had never heard the name Erwin, and he didn't like that name. He wanted a more common name such as John or Joe or Bill.

He came to the States, and over the years he moved with his mother from state to state. He could have changed his name anytime, but he wouldn't. As much as he didn't care for his new name, Erwin, what made him keep it was that that was the only time he'd ever heard anyone say that he was going to do something great. His teachers, counselors, and grandfather had never encouraged him, but that day he heard that he would change the world, that he would be a person of valor and honor, that the name was for a genius. He knew the negative that was said about him, but now someone was saying that he was exceptional, that he had greatness in him. Every time he was tempted to shrink back and accept mediocrity, he would remember what his grandfather had said the name Erwin represented. Today, our friend Erwin McManus is an amazing pastor, author, filmmaker. He is one of the brightest minds around.

I wonder if we would have ever heard of Erwin; I wonder if his gifts and talents would have ever come out, if he had not changed his name. What if his grandfather had not reminded him of who he really was, not who people said he was, not who the experts said he was, not who the environment said he was, but who God said he was—a son of

> *What if his grandfather had not reminded him of who he really was, not who people said he was, not who the experts said he was, not who the environment said he was, but who God said he was— a son of strength, talented, creative, one of a kind, with seeds of greatness?*

strength, talented, creative, one of a kind, with seeds of greatness? Like Erwin, maybe nobody has told you who you really are. Life has put some names on you and told you what you're not, what you can't do, how you're at a disadvantage, how you've made too many mistakes. God has you hearing this because He wants you to change your name. No more answering to mediocre, not talented enough, born to lose. There is greatness in you. God created you in His own image. He put a part of Himself in you. You've been equipped, empowered, and anointed. He crowned you with His favor. Your new name is blessed, prosperous, confident, healthy, free, well able, victorious.

ACCEPT THE NAME CHANGE

When God promised Abraham and Sarah that they were going to have a baby, they were way too old. In the natural, it was impossible. But God didn't just give them the promise, He changed their names. In Genesis 17, God said, "No longer will you be called Abram, your name will be Abraham," which means "a father of many nations." When God changed his name, he didn't have a child with Sarah, yet every time someone said, "Hello, Abraham," they were saying, "Hello, father of many nations." They were speaking faith into his destiny. Abraham heard that again and again. What you continually hear starts to get down inside. You will become what you believe. That's why it's so important to have the right names. "I am blessed. I am prosperous. I am healthy." "But, Joel, I don't feel healthy." Keep calling yourself that. That's what allows it to happen. "I don't feel blessed. I'm struggling. I'm in debt. I'll never get ahead." You're right where Abraham was. He could have said, "I don't have my promised child. I'm too old. My wife has gone through the change of life." God changed his name so he would hear it again and again: "You're the father of many nations."

You may not feel blessed. You're tempted to complain and talk about what you don't have and how it's not going to get better. That's why you're hearing this. God is changing your name from lack, struggle, can't get ahead to blessed, prosperous, more than enough. Now you have to start calling yourself

> *What you continually hear starts to get down inside. You will become what you believe.*

what God says about you. The change may not happen overnight, but every time you call yourself by what God named you, it's getting deeper inside, it's changing your self-image, it's reprogramming your mind. I'm sure there were times when Abraham thought, *We'll never have a child.* About that time someone would walk up and call his name, "Hey, Abraham." He would be reminded, "You're the father of many nations." You have to call yourself blessed before you'll ever be blessed. You have to call yourself healthy while you're still fighting that sickness. Call yourself free while you're still struggling with the addiction. Having the right name is what's going to help you stay strong so you can become what God says about you.

God also changed Sarah's name from Sarai to Sarah, which means "princess." If anyone didn't feel like a princess, it would have been Sarah. She had been barren for nearly ninety years. She didn't feel attractive or special. Everything told her she was finished. She could never have a baby. It was too late. She could have said, "Don't change my name. Call me Sarai. I'm not a princess. That's not going to make any difference." But she accepted the name change. She said, in effect, "This doesn't seem possible, the odds are against me, but if God says I'm a princess, I'm going to get in agreement with Him." Every time someone said, "Good morning, Sarah," they were saying, "Good morning, Princess." She heard that so many times that something began to come alive inside. Faith began to rise up. She started believing. That's when God stepped in and brought the promise to pass.

You may have situations that you don't see how it could work out in your health, your finances, a relationship. What you're up against looks permanent. Like with Abraham and Sarah, God is changing your name. You've had that addiction for years, but God is calling you free. You've not been able to have children, but God is calling you a mother. He's calling your womb blessed. You're fighting a sickness and don't feel well, but God is changing your name to healthy and whole. Your dream seems too big, you don't have the funds, the training, or the experience, but God is calling you successful. He's calling you abundant, bountiful, and prosperous. Now the whole key is, will you do like Abraham and Sarah and accept the name change? Will you call yourself what God calls you when it seems like it doesn't make sense? Every time you do that, it's getting stronger inside. Like them, you're going to become what you believe.

DON'T LET "THEY" NAME YOU

In Luke 1, an angel appeared to Zechariah and told him that his wife, Elizabeth, was going to have a baby, whom they were to name John. They were both very old, and Elizabeth had never been able to conceive. Zechariah asked the angel how it could happen. The angel assured him that what God promised would come to pass, but because Zechariah doubted, he would remain silent until the baby was born. From that moment on, he couldn't speak. Nine months later, Elizabeth gave birth to a baby boy. Their friends and relatives came to the house to celebrate, and the Scripture says, "They wanted to name the baby Zechariah after his father." God said his name was John, but "they" wanted to name him something different. We all have "they" people in our lives. Neighbors, coworkers, and relatives will try to name you something that you're not. Sometimes they are well-meaning. When my father was a teenager, his parents

> *We all have "they" people in our lives. Neighbors, coworkers, and relatives will try to name you something that you're not.*

told him that he couldn't become a minister, that all he knew how to do was pick cotton. God named him a pastor, but "they" named him not talented, below par, mediocre. If my father had accepted their names, he wouldn't have impacted the world. People will name you average, unqualified, not attractive, wrong nationality. Don't let "they" name you; let God name you. When "they" said his name would be Zechariah, Elizabeth said, "No! His name will be John." "They" said, "What do you mean? There's no one in your family named John. That doesn't make sense." "They" went to ask Zechariah, but he still couldn't speak. He wrote down on a tablet, "His name is John," and suddenly he could speak again.

Back in those days, women didn't have the influence that they have today, and mothers were not allowed to name their babies. The grandparents, the friends, and the neighbors also couldn't name the child. The only one who had the authority to name the baby was the father. They had to go to Zechariah and find out what the baby's name would be. Your Heavenly Father is the only One who has the right to name you.

> *Your Heavenly Father is the only One who has the right to name you.*

Have you let "they" people name you? Have you let circumstances tell you who you are or let negative thoughts convince you that you've seen your best days? Like God did for Abraham and Sarah, I believe He's changing your name right now. Now do your part and accept the name change. Tune out all the negatives and keep calling yourself what God calls you. When you do, you will step into new levels of influence, favor, opportunity, promotion, healing, and breakthroughs.

CHAPTER FOUR

Build Yourself Up

When you know who you are and where you get your value from and you've approved yourself, whether you have other people's approval or disapproval does not faze you.

It's good to have people who cheer us on and speak faith into our life. It's good to have a spouse who compliments us, a neighbor with an uplifting word, a friend who's always there to encourage. It's healthy when you have people who make you feel valued and appreciated. But it becomes unhealthy if you start depending on them to keep you cheered up. If they don't compliment you, you don't feel good about who you are. If they're not there to encourage you, you don't have any passion. If your coworker doesn't tell you that you did good on a project, you're down, thinking you're not enough. We can become addicted to approval and compliments to where we base our value, our worth, on what people are telling us. It's like a drug—we need them to feel good about who we are. But God didn't create you to be dependent on someone else to keep you fixed. He uses people to encourage and uplift, but at some point He's going to pull them back. He's not going to let them keep giving you that, or else you'll get stuck.

The problem with relying on others is that they can let you down. People can be busy, and they're not there when you need them. They are dealing with their own issues. They're raising their children, struggling in their marriage or their work. If you're counting on others to call you every morning and prop you up, or to tell you how good you look at work, or to encourage you in a difficulty, that's a codependent relationship. You need them to feel good about who you are. Here's a key: If nobody is complimenting you, you need to learn to compliment yourself. If nobody told you that you look good today, why don't you look in the mirror and say, "Wow, you look good! You're a treasure, one of a kind, a prized possession." If nobody made you feel special, if your friend didn't call, if your neighbor didn't come over, here's the good news: You can make yourself feel special. Just say, "I'm a child of the Most High God. I've been handpicked by the Creator of the universe. I have royal blood flowing through my veins."

> *Quit putting how you feel about yourself, your value, and your mood in someone else's hands.*

Quit putting how you feel about yourself, your value, and your mood in someone else's hands. The Scripture says, "Build yourself up." Don't rely on other people to affirm, to approve, to validate you. Approve yourself. Tell yourself, "I'm made in the image of Almighty God. I'm approved. I'm worthy. I'm valuable." When you're trying to get your approval, your validation, from other people, you're at their mercy. If they're having a bad day, if they're upset and mad at their spouse, you're not going to get what you were hoping for from them. But when you learn to build yourself up, what they give or don't give doesn't affect you. You're already built up. You already know who you are. Keep building yourself up. As you continue strengthening your inner life, you'll begin reclaiming the extraordinary life you were created to live. You don't need other people to keep you fixed, because you encourage yourself. You compliment yourself. You approve yourself. This is a powerful way to live. Nobody else is controlling your mood, controlling your self-worth. You've taken control.

TUNE OUT THE INNER CRITIC

Every morning before you leave the house, you need to build yourself up. Don't go out the door hoping to get encouraged, hoping someone makes you feel good. *Maybe my friend will cheer me up. Maybe my coworker will compliment me on my presentation and make me feel valuable.* They don't control your value. Don't give them that power. If you're trying to get those things from people, you're going to live on an emotional roller coaster. One day people love you, and the next day they're talking behind your back. One day your friend is full of compliments, the next day they're full of a lot of other stuff. One day your wife is so encouraging and uplifting, the next day she's worried about something or in a stressed out mood.

When you build yourself up, you're not moved by the negative chatter. You're not bitter over who didn't give you credit. You're not frustrated because people didn't approve you. You already approved yourself. Nobody said anything good about all your hard work, but that's okay. You already complimented yourself. Nobody clapped for your excellent presentation. The ones who should have been so encouraging, so happy for you, instead got jealous. They found fault. That's okay. You already clapped for yourself. They didn't celebrate you, but you celebrated yourself. "Father, thank You for helping me to shine. Thank You for my gifts,

> **When you build yourself up, you're not moved by the negative chatter.**

my talents, and for causing me to excel." You're not dependent on what others do to feel good about who you are.

Every time I finish a message and walk off the platform, I say under my breath, "Joel, you did good today. That was excellent." I don't mean that arrogantly, but I've learned to celebrate myself. It may not have been as good as what someone else could do. There are ministers who are far more skilled and experienced than me, but I gave to the best of my ability. It's healthy to clap for yourself, to celebrate what you've done. You're not bragging on you. You're bragging on the gifts, the talents, the abilities that God has given you. For some people, no matter what they do, it's never good enough. There's always a nagging voice saying, "You should have done better." They live with an inner critic that's constantly putting them down, pointing out faults, magnifying the negative. "You gave a good message, Joel, but it was a little slow at times. You worked out four days this week, but you really should have done five. You look okay today, but not like you used to look." Do yourself a favor and tune out that inner critic.

You have enough people trying to push you down, limit your potential, and lessen your value. You don't need another critical voice inside you.

> *Nobody should be more for you than you.*

Nobody should be more for you than you. That's not being selfish. That's being responsible with the gifts God has given you. Learn to celebrate yourself. You clap for others. When was the last time you clapped for yourself? You compliment your friends. When was the last time you complimented yourself? You brag on your coworker, "That was excellent. You did great." When was the last time you bragged on you and told yourself, "You did great"? It's healthy to clap for you. The more you applaud yourself, the less dependent you are on other people's applause. If you approve yourself, you're not going to be needy for other people's approval. If you are free with your compliments to yourself, you won't be insecure, trying to play up to people to win their compliments, get them to validate you, and tell you that you're good. You won't need that. You've already built yourself up with who God says you are. You know you're valuable, you're worthy, you're talented. You're attractive and you're exceptional. It's nice when people reaffirm that, but you're not dependent on it to feel good about who you are. You know who you are.

RIVERS OF LIVING WATER

After one of our church services, I was talking to a man who was very nice, but he said, "Joel, I just didn't understand that one point you made in your message. It didn't make sense to me." If I had heard that during the first couple of years I had been ministering, I would have gone home defeated, feeling inadequate, and been depressed for two months. But I've learned what I'm telling you, that I didn't need his applause. I had already clapped for myself. I wasn't basing my joy, my worth, or my confidence on what he did or didn't give me. I had already built myself up. Yes, I'm always open for suggestions. There are things we all can do better, but you're never going to please everyone. No matter how good you do, someone is going to find fault, try to discredit you, or not give their approval. I love what Jesus said to some religious leaders who had criticized Him for healing a sick man on the Sabbath: "Your approval or disapproval means nothing to me." He wasn't being disrespectful. He was simply saying, "I know who I am, and I know where I get my value." That's the place we need to get to. We don't have to have people's approval to feel good about who we are. Sure, there will be people who disapprove and criticize, but that doesn't faze us. We don't get defensive and try to straighten them out. We don't get discouraged and go around feeling less-than. We keep our shoulders back. We know who we are. They didn't approve us, but we've approved ourselves. They didn't compliment us, but we complimented ourselves. Nobody clapped for us, but that didn't change our worth. We clapped for ourselves.

When that man told me that he didn't understand my point, I didn't take it personally. I didn't let it ruin my day. When you're built up inside, that's going to protect you from what comes on the outside. The first thing I do every morning, after I thank God for what He's done, is to remind myself of who I am. "Lord, thank You that You chose me before I could choose You. Thank You that I am a person of destiny, redeemed and forgiven. You've made me worthy. You've accepted me and approved me, You've crowned me with favor and put a robe of righteousness on me. You've planned out my days for good." I never leave the house without building myself up. That way I'm not waiting for someone else to build me up. I'm not hoping that Victoria says something to cheer me up. I'm not hoping my coworker claps for me, so I'll feel valuable. I'm not hoping my friend compliments me, so I'll be secure. No, quit depending on people. That's no way to live. That's putting your self-worth and your mood into their hands. Put it in God's hands. Go to Him to get your value, your approval.

The Scripture says, "Out of your belly shall flow rivers of living water," meaning God has put amazing things in you, and He wants that to flow out—dreams, businesses, books, inventions, and talent. We're looking to others to keep us filled up, to keep us encouraged, to keep us secure, to keep us feeling valuable. Here's a key: Nobody can give you everything you need. Nobody can keep you fixed. Your spouse, your friends, and your boss may love you more than anything, be totally for you, but only God can give you what you need. He'll use people, but people are limited. If you're depending on another person, it's not only going to frustrate you but it puts a lot of pressure on them. When they take that weight, thinking, *I have to call and encourage him, be there to cheer him up and approve him. I can't let him down*, that's a load they can't carry. You're trying to

> *Nobody can give you everything you need. Nobody can keep you fixed.*

get from them what only God can give. The sooner you start building yourself up, the better off it's going to be for you and the other people in your life. You weren't created to live relying on someone else, basing your worth on who approves you. Approve yourself. Turn off that inner critic that's always putting you down. You're supposed to feel good about who you are. We all have flaws, areas where we need to make improvements. But you don't have to wait until you're perfect to feel worthy and approved.

> *You're supposed to feel good about who you are.*

YOU ARE ALREADY APPROVED

In Genesis 1, the Earth was without form and void. God said, "Let there be light," and light came. God saw the light and said, "That was good." He stopped and clapped for Himself. What's interesting is that there were no planets, no oceans, no animals, no people. He wasn't finished. There were still a lot of things that needed to be done, but He didn't wait until it was all complete. He celebrated along the way. On the second day, God separated the waters

Build Yourself Up

from the sky. He still hadn't made any fish. There still were no mountain ranges or sunsets. But at the end of the day, God said, "That was good." He stopped and applauded, complimented Himself. Same thing after day three, day four, day five. Even though it wasn't finished, He said it was good.

The truth is none of us are finished products. God is still working on us. But even though we have things we need to improve in, you shouldn't feel unworthy, go around down on yourself, trying to get people to approve you. God has already approved you. He's already accepted you. Why don't you start believing that you're worthy, that you're valuable? The enemy would love for you to feel unworthy when, in fact, the Creator of the universe applauded you. Why don't you start building yourself up, declaring who God says you are?

> *Even though we have things we need to improve in, you shouldn't feel unworthy, go around down on yourself, trying to get people to approve you.*

It's going to limit you if you're basing your joy, your attitude, your self-worth on who compliments you, who claps for you, who thinks you're attractive. Can I tell you that you don't need their applause? You can clap for yourself. You don't need their compliments. You can compliment yourself. Out of your belly shall flow rivers of living water. In some people, that river is stopped up. They've lived their whole lives trying to gain approval, earn their value, and convince people to clap for them. They live frustrated, letting people manipulate them, and are down on themselves because they're not getting the applause. Today can be a turning point. Quit looking to people and start going to God. Nobody is congratulating you on your promotion, so learn to congratulate yourself. Nobody is buying you flowers, so buy yourself some flowers. Nobody is taking you to dinner, so take yourself to dinner.

I know a young woman who didn't have a lot of friends when she was in junior high. She had just moved to a new school where most of the students had grown up together and been friends for years. She couldn't seem to break in and really connect with anyone. During Valentine's week, the school had a tradition where you could send another student a carnation for just twenty-five cents. They would be delivered during homeroom on Valentine's Day in front of the whole class. Because she didn't know anyone yet, she knew she wasn't going to receive any carnations and was dreading that day, knowing she was going to feel

Build Yourself Up

left out and embarrassed by it all. Then she came up with an idea. She decided to send herself some flowers. She took five dollars, went to the office, and got twenty different forms so nobody would know it was the same person. On Valentine's Day, most of the girls got four or five carnations, and the most popular girl got seven. But this young lady had every other carnation delivered to her. The kids in her class were thinking, *Who is that girl? She has so many friends.* They asked, "Who's this one from?" She smiled and said, "From someone who really thinks I'm special." You celebrate others, but do you ever celebrate yourself? You're good to your friends. You encourage and build them up. Do you ever build yourself up? It's not selfish to be good to you. The more you applaud yourself, the less dependent you are on other people's applause, and the more secure you're going to be.

> *You celebrate others, but do you ever celebrate yourself?*

YOU NEED TO BE FOR YOU

I have a pastor friend in another state who used to call me every Sunday afternoon. He would speak at his two services that morning, then come home and watch the replay of my message online. He was always so encouraging, so uplifting. He would tell me how good I did, how impactful it was, the points he really liked, and on and on. You would think I was the greatest pastor ever. That was his personality. His whole nature was to build others up. But he told me later that he would drive home every Sunday from his church thinking about how he didn't do good. "That was too long. That wasn't clear. I forgot to say this." He said, "I never left my church one time feeling good about myself. I always went home disappointed." He knew how to compliment others, but he didn't know how to compliment himself. He clapped for me all the time, was my biggest cheerleader, but he never clapped for himself. He was great at building me up, making me feel valuable, well able, but he never built himself up. He listened to that inner critic always finding fault, condemning, pushing him down.

Don't go your whole life being good to others, encouraging others, but never being good to you, never encouraging you. Don't go around thinking highly of your friends, but not thinking highly of you. It's good to applaud others, but you have to learn to clap for yourself. They may be more successful, have more talent, be more attractive, but you have something they don't have. You are unique. You are one of a kind. Don't discount who you are. God didn't make anything second-class or subpar. He calls you a masterpiece. When He created the solar system, He said it was good. He said the mountain ranges and oceans were good. But when God breathed life into you, He said that was *very* good. Put your shoulders back. Hold your head high. When you clap for yourself, you're clapping for your Creator. When you compliment yourself, you're complimenting the God who made you. When you build yourself up, you're saying, "God, thank You for who I am. I am blessed, strong, talented, worthy, and victorious." That's giving praise to God.

> *God didn't make anything second-class or subpar. He calls you a masterpiece.*

Several years after my pastor friend began calling me with encouragement, Victoria and I were with him and another friend. I had just finished a live interview on a national network, a big deal. We got in the car afterward, and I looked at them and said, "Wow, y'all, I did really good. I don't think I could have done any better." I wasn't bragging. I was just grateful that I had done well. I didn't think twice about saying that. My pastor friend told me later that moment changed his life. He had never once said to himself that he had done good. He'd grown up with a negative recording playing in his mind. When he heard me be positive toward myself, a stronghold was broken in his thinking. He started applauding himself, approving himself, encouraging himself. You have enough people in life against you; don't be against yourself. You need to be for you. You won't reach your destiny letting that inner critic always put you down. That causes you to feel inferior and insecure, and it leads you to trying to get approval and applause from those around you, depending on them to keep you fixed. You can fix yourself. Every morning, remind yourself who God says you are. Don't rely on other people. Build yourself up.

> *You have enough people in life against you; don't be against yourself.*

OTHERS' APPROVAL IS TEMPORARY PROVISION

When I first started ministering, I was very insecure and intimidated. I had been behind the scenes working on the television production for seventeen years. I liked it there. I was comfortable, but now I was out front. I was so unsure of myself at first that I lived off of people's compliments. After the service, people would tell me, "Joel, that was so good today. I really enjoyed your message." Those words helped give me the strength and confidence to keep going. When I would get up to minister during that first year, people would cheer and cheer. They were so loyal to my parents, and they wanted me to succeed so badly that they poured all their encouragement and support into me. I could have talked about Moses defeating Goliath, about David parting the Red Sea, getting it all backward, but they still would have cheered. God knew that I needed that external applause, that outside validation and approval to keep going. God will make sure that you have what you need for every stage of your journey. There are times when you need others speaking encouragement into your life, helping you to stay built up. But at some point, God is going to remove that so it doesn't become a crutch. He'll let you rely on others to keep you encouraged, to depend on your friends to keep you cheered up, to rely on your family to keep you feeling valuable, but that's temporary provision. Like a mother weans a baby off the bottle, God is going

> *Like a mother weans a baby off the bottle, God is going to wean you off the external approval, the external applause.*

to wean you off the external approval, the external applause. You have to learn to get that from the inside. Remember, out of your belly shall flow rivers. Instead of depending on others, you become self-sufficient. That's what the apostle Paul says in Philippians 4: "I am self-sufficient in Christ's sufficiency." When you go to God, you're not dependent on others.

The first few years, every time I finished my message and walked off the platform, Victoria would say, "Joel, that was amazing today. You did so good." She would always compliment me and make me feel encouraged. I looked forward to it. I knew, like clockwork, Victoria would have a kind, uplifting word. I didn't realize that's where I was getting my validation, my approval, from people telling me I did good. One day, I walked off the platform and Victoria didn't say a word. I waited and waited. She started asking me about something else. I answered quickly, then kind of hinted about the message, trying to pull a compliment out. Unfortunately, she didn't get the hint. She turned and went the other way. I thought,

Maybe she's just preoccupied, has something else on her mind. I went to the lobby, shook hands with several hundred visitors, and not one of them said anything about my message. Usually, every other visitor, just being courteous, says, "Joel, that was so good." The funny thing is, I knew it was a good message. I was confident. But I was waiting for someone else to tell me. I needed outside approval to feel good about it.

I left the church that day so discouraged. Whenever I get home, our dog hears the garage door opening and is always at the back door, jumping up on me, so happy to see me. That's one thing I can count on. But that day, when I opened the door, the dog was lying in her bed. She didn't even get up. She turned her head and looked at me for about three seconds, then turned and looked away, like she was saying, "Oh, it's just you." She rolled over and went back to sleep.

What was happening? God was weaning me off having to have compliments and approval and validation from the outside. There may be seasons when you're getting that, but don't be surprised if God pulls it back. You can't reach your highest potential depending on others. It's great when people compliment you, but it's even more powerful when you compliment yourself. It's nice when they applaud,

> *You can't reach your highest potential depending on others.*

they approve, they validate, but the problem is you can't depend on people. If they're keeping you fixed, that's temporary. God didn't create you to have to rely on someone else for your self-worth, your approval, or even your encouragement. At some point, you're going to have to learn to encourage yourself. God is growing you up. He's getting you ready for higher levels. The less you depend on other people, the more mature you are. My challenge to you is, start building yourself up. Nobody is clapping; start clapping for yourself. No one is approving you; approve yourself. You don't have to go to people; go to your Heavenly Father, the God who made you. Let Him breathe strength, value, favor, freedom, and healing in you. If you do this, chains of insecurity, low self-esteem, and unworthiness will be broken. You will rise to higher levels and accomplish your dreams.

CHAPTER FIVE

Get Your Mind Going in the Right Direction

God has made you a new creation, the new you, but there remains this battle between who you are called to be and who you used to be, between the flesh and the spirit.

We each have two sides to our nature. There is the strong, disciplined, confident side of you and the weak, insecure, compromising side of you. There's the nice, kind, compassionate you and the critical, rude, judgmental you. There's the positive, faith-filled, big-dreams you and the negative, discouraged, never-going-to-happen you. We all have these contradictions, these inconsistencies. You're a good person, you love the Lord, and most of the time you're kind, happy, and easygoing. You say, "Good morning. How are you today? It's great to see you." But if somebody pushes the right buttons—if they're rude, hurtful, and critical—the other you comes out. He might have been hidden for two months, you might have even thought he was finally gone, but he was still in there. There's a battle constantly taking place inside between the two yous.

The Scripture calls it the battle between the flesh and the spirit. It's the battle between the new redeemed

> *The old you may be dead, but sometimes he gets resurrected. He may have died, but don't kid yourself: He can get back up again.*

nature and the old carnal nature that gives in to our feelings, compromises, tells somebody off, and is lazy. When you gave your life to Christ, the apostle Paul says, "If any man be in Christ, he is a new creation; old things have passed away." We celebrate that as good news. But what I've learned is that the old you may be dead, but sometimes he gets resurrected. He may have died, but don't kid yourself: He can get back up again.

A NEW CREATION, BUT...

We already saw this displayed in Peter's life. He was a faithful disciple, a close friend of Jesus, strong, and committed. His name even means "rock." There was no one whom Jesus had more confidence in than Peter. When the soldiers came to arrest Jesus, Peter was so loyal, so determined that he was ready to die defending Christ with a sword. That was the strong Peter, the faithful Peter, the rock. It would have been great if that was the only Peter, but there was another side to Peter who came out from time to time.

When they arrested Jesus and took Him to the high priest, Peter followed at a distance. He was standing in the courtyard, warming himself by the

Get Your Mind Going in the Right Direction

fire, while Jesus was inside being questioned. There were guards all around when a young lady said to Peter, "Aren't you one of Jesus' disciples?" Peter said, "No. What are you talking about? I don't know Him." Another person came up and said, "Are you sure you're not one of His disciples?" Peter said it again, "I'm telling you, I don't know Him." Later, one of the servants of the high priest asked, "I saw you in the garden when we arrested Him. I know you're one of His disciples." This time Peter got angry, and he began to curse and swear, "I don't know the Man." Just a little earlier he had been defending Jesus. What happened? Peter's old nature—the curse-you-out, deny-you Peter—got back up and tried to rule his new nature, the kind, loyal Peter.

I'd love to tell you that you don't have a battle going on inside of you. I'd love to tell you that you're not like Peter, that you don't still have the rude you, the compromising you, the curse-you-out you living inside you, but that's not the truth. We all have the other me in us. We are a new creation, but the flesh, even though it's passed away, can get back up. In Romans 8, Paul says, "If you live by the flesh you will die." It's not talking

> **We all have the other me in us.**

about dying physically; it means your dreams will die, your potential will die, your relationships will not be what they should be. If you live according to the flesh, you're always popping off, saying what you want to say, holding grudges, being unfaithful, and compromising. It feels good to feed the flesh, but you won't like the results. You won't get to where you're supposed to be. Paul goes on to say, "But if through the Spirit, you mortify the flesh, then you will live." *Mortify* means you have to keep it dead. When it tries to get up, when you're tempted to do whatever you feel, you have to dig your heels in and say, "No, I'm not going to let the flesh rule me." When you do the right thing when it's uncomfortable, you're keeping the old man down. Keep your thoughts going in the right direction—let God guide you along the best path to rediscovering the forgotten you. When your mind is set on hope and purpose, your life will follow in that same powerful direction.

DON'T LET THE OLD YOU GET BACK UP

The writer of Hebrews says, "No discipline seems pleasant at the time, but painful. Later on, it will produce a harvest of righteousness." When somebody insults you, it doesn't feel good to walk away. What feels good is to immediately insult them back. It doesn't feel good to not give in to the temptation to watch something you shouldn't, to not gossip about a friend, to not be lazy but instead study for a test. The flesh likes to be comfortable. It likes to take the easy way. But you don't grow when you're always comfortable. The reason some people are stuck, don't have healthy relationships, and aren't being promoted is not because they don't have God's favor, not because they're not talented; it's because they keep letting the old man get up. They're not disciplined to do the right thing when it's hard. You have to be consistent. The flesh is not going to go away. You'll never become so spiritual that you don't have to deal with the flesh. The apostle Paul said, "I die daily." He wrote nearly half the books of the New Testament, yet he had to deal with his flesh on a daily basis. Every day we have to say no to things. "No, I'm not going to watch that. No, I'm not going to make that sarcastic remark. No, I'm not going to stay home and play on the computer all day. No, I'm not going to hang out with that friend who causes me to compromise."

You have to tell the flesh: "You are not going to

rule me. I'm not going to eat everything you tell me to eat." At the mall, you can smell those fresh baked cinnamon rolls just around the corner. Before you exit the freeway, that aroma is already in the air. Your new you says, "Keep walking by. You don't need that sugar." The old you may be dead, but he can still smell. He gets up and says, "You need three of those. You deserve it. You can work out extra hard tomorrow. You can pray and ask God to take the calories away. Give me what I want." It's similar to what happened to Peter around the fire; this is just in a more practical light. Instead of the kind you versus the cursing you, it's the healthy you versus the eat-everything-I-want you. You've heard of the walking dead. Your old man is dead, but he'll get up and walk around. He'll try to control your life.

> *The old you may be dead, but he can still smell.*

> *Every time you compromise, every time you become impatient, every time you get offended, you're feeding the negative.*

Now quit telling yourself, "I can't control my temper. I can't break this addiction. I can't keep my eyes on the right things." Your old you is not that strong. The reason he's controlling you is you keep feeding him. Whatever you feed is going to grow. Every time you give in to that temptation, you're feeding it. It's getting stronger. Every time you compromise, every time you become impatient, every time you get offended, you're feeding the negative. Do yourself a favor and quit feeding the old you. You have to start starving the temptation by not giving in, starving the temper by biting your tongue, starving the bad attitude, the offense, the bitterness. When you starve the negative, it's going to get weaker.

"Joel, I've tried to do it, but I just don't have the discipline." You're defeating yourself in your own thinking. That battle starts in our mind. In Philippians 2, the apostle Paul says, "God is working in you, giving you the desire to obey Him and the power to do what is right." Right now, the Most High God is working in you. He's bigger than any temptation, bigger than any stronghold. He created you to be free. Instead of going through the day thinking, *I can't break this addiction. I'll never control my temper. I'll never resist this temptation*, turn it around and say, "Father, thank You that You're giving me the desire to obey You. Thank You that I have the power to overcome, that the forces for me are greater than the forces against me." Get your mind going in the right direction. That's the first step to victory.

WHAT ARE YOUR PERSONAL ENEMIES?

David had to do the right thing and choose the new man in himself before God could trust him to accomplish a great victory in front of a crowd and defeat Goliath. Goliath, in one sense, was not David's enemy; he was God's enemy. Goliath was there to establish the Israelites, to let the Philistines know that God was on the Israelites' side. When David was out alone in the shepherds' fields, when nobody was watching, he killed the lion and the bear with his own hands. He could have slacked off and thought, *Nobody is watching. Nobody will know if I lose a sheep or two. It's no big deal. Why should I care?* But David was a person of excellence. He did his best when nobody was watching. Because David was faithful in his own battles, God was able to promote him and use him to defeat His enemies. You have to do what David did and start fighting, and winning, your personal battles, the things nobody knows about. It may be a sin, or just a weight, just a small thing that's keeping you from being your best. It may be a sour attitude, being late to work, or being jealous of a friend. Are there personal battles you're not dealing with? You're allowing them to stay because you think it's not that big a deal, just something everybody struggles with. It's time to put the old you back in the grave. He's been up too long. If you deal with the small things that are holding you back, God will release the big things that belong to you.

> *If you deal with the small things that are holding you back, God will release the big things that belong to you.*

Sometimes we're waiting for the struggle to totally go away, thinking that God is going to take away the desire; we're not going to have the temptation anymore, we're not going to feel upset when somebody says something offensive. There are times when God totally takes away the desire, but most of the time the desire is still going to be there, and the old you is still going to try to get back up. But God gives you the grace to overcome. He gives you the power to do the right thing.

I've always been very focused, very goal oriented. If I'm going to the grocery store, I'm on a mission.

I'm going to get in and get out quickly and efficiently. I don't like to wait around. I used to be impatient, but I wouldn't let anyone see it. I would be stressed if there was a long checkout line or if the waiter didn't show up at the table right away. But living with Victoria has taught me to slow down, enjoy my life, and not be in a hurry. I'm much more at ease, go with the flow, and don't let things upset me. But even now, when things aren't moving fast enough, when the person on the freeway in front of me is driving forty in the fast lane, the old me still wants to get up. I've had him down for years. We buried him, had a funeral, but every week he's trying to get back up.

What I'm saying is that God doesn't take away every negative desire to where you're never going to be tempted to be impatient again, never have the desire to be critical, rude, judgmental, or to compromise. That's why the apostle Paul said, "I die daily." You still have the desire to get off course and join the crowd. That's where discipline steps in. That's where the grace of God shows up. Yes, I know people whom God delivered from an addiction, and they don't have any desire to do it again. That happens, that's the mercy of God. But if it doesn't happen that way for you, don't let it be an excuse to let your old man back up. Keep the old you in the grave. He doesn't look good on you. He's not your style. Keep the old you down, so the new you can shine.

EVERY PERSON HAS A SAUL

Here's what I've learned. Anything you defeat quickly is not your real enemy. What you overcome in a short time is not what you have to be concerned with. Thank God for it, but your real enemy doesn't go away easily. I'm not tempted to curse, to do drugs, to be dishonest. By the grace of God, I don't struggle in those areas. But dealing with impatience, that old me has been trying to get up for over thirty years. He's stubborn. He won't go away. For me, he's a real enemy. When David defeated Goliath in a matter of minutes, it was a victory that changed the course of his life. But Goliath wasn't his real enemy; he was gone in a moment. King Saul was David's real enemy. For years he pestered David, threw spears at him when David was being nice.

> *Anything you defeat quickly is not your real enemy.*

He chased David through the desert trying to kill him. David had to live on the run. God could have delivered David from Saul like He did with Goliath. He could have taken care of him in one afternoon; no big deal. But there are some enemies, some temptations, some desires that God doesn't remove. If He doesn't remove it, if He doesn't take it totally away, that means He's given you the grace to stand strong. You have the power to not let the old you get back up.

> *You have the power to not let the old you get back up.*

You may be tempted to hold on to bitterness after somebody hurt you or did you wrong. It's been years and that temptation, that desire, hasn't gone away. That's your real enemy. Keep the old you down. Do the right thing when it's hard and when nobody else is watching. Bitterness doesn't look good on you. Maybe you have an ongoing temptation with alcohol, or to be unfaithful in a relationship, or to be negative and critical. You've dealt with this for years. Every person has a Saul. There will be a temptation, an attitude, or some area of compromise that God doesn't exempt us from. You need to understand what your real enemy is and where your real battle lies. Don't let the Sauls wear you down to where you start giving in, thinking, *This is just who I am.* No; announce to Saul, "You're not going to keep me from my purpose. If you never go away, I'm not giving in. I'm not letting the old me back up. I'm going to keep resisting, standing strong, doing the right thing." Don't let your Saul keep you from your destiny.

Human nature wants a quick fix. "God, deliver me instantly. Take this temper away. Keep my mouth shut. Make me patient and kind. Lord, do it overnight." You'll defeat some giants overnight. God will help you conquer a few Goliaths quickly, but most of the time God will deliver you little by little. It's when He sees you doing your part, being patient when you feel stressed, keeping a good attitude when you didn't get your way, saying no to the temptation, forgiving the person who did you wrong. As you keep passing the tests, God will release more of His favor. One step at a time, He'll change things.

> *God will help you conquer a few Goliaths quickly, but most of the time God will deliver you little by little.*

IS IT JACOB OR ISRAEL?

In the Scripture, this is what happened with Jacob. He was dishonest, went around deceiving people, and tricked his brother out of his birthright. Dishonesty was Jacob's Saul. He struggled with it for years. He wasn't disciplined, didn't try to overcome it, just accepted it as who he was. But in Genesis 32, after he wrestled with an angel, God changed his name from Jacob, which means "a deceiver," to Israel, which means "a prince with God." This was to signify his new beginning. God was saying, "Jacob, I'm giving you the grace to conquer this dishonesty. You can bury the old you." Jacob did his best to change and live a life of integrity. He started making better choices and treating people right. But just because God touched him didn't mean that Jacob suddenly turned into another person and no longer had the temptation, the desires, he struggled with before. We see this in Genesis 48 when he came to the end of his life and it says, "When Jacob was told, 'Your son Joseph is here to see you,' Israel gathered his strength and sat up in the bed." He was near death and look who was there—Jacob and Israel. You would think the Scripture would just refer to him by Israel, his new name. Wasn't Jacob over and done? But this was put there to show us that he never totally got rid of Jacob. He lived as Israel, that was his new name, but Jacob didn't let go easily. He kept trying to come back again and again.

It's the same with us. God has made us a new creation. He says you're no longer Jacob, no longer the compromiser, the deceiver; you are Israel, a prince with God. But even though you're Israel, Jacob is going to get up out of that grave and try to work his way back. There will be this conflict between the two men, who you're called to be and who you used to be. When you get cut off in traffic, Israel will say, "No big deal. It's not going to ruin my day. Bless them, Lord." It would be easy if Jacob was totally gone. The problem is that Jacob is still in there. When Israel says, "I'm going to bless them," Jacob will get up and say, "No, I'm going to curse them." When you find yourself wanting to compromise, to be impatient, to give in to the temptation, just say to yourself, "No, Jacob, you're not getting

> *There will be this conflict between the two men, who you're called to be and who you used to be.*

up. You're done. You're the old me. Stay in the grave. Israel is in charge. The redeemed me, the free me, the blessed me rules."

THE REFINING PROCESS

"Joel, it's hard to take the high road. It's hard to keep my mouth closed when somebody does me wrong. It's hard to resist the temptation." Yes, it's difficult, but you won't come up higher if you're not willing to be uncomfortable. Those are tests that God allows so you can grow. The Scripture talks about how God uses difficulties to separate the wheat from the chaff. The chaff is the unusable part of the plant. If you don't get rid of the unnecessary parts, the valuable part will go to waste. In Bible days, they would take the wheat sheaves to a threshing floor where oxen would walk over it again and again. The threshing process broke the valuable grains loose from the husks and straw. Then the chaff would be separated from the grain by lifting the threshed

> *You won't come up higher if you're not willing to be uncomfortable.*

wheat into the air, and the wind would carry away the chaff.

When you're in a situation that you don't like, when you're uncomfortable, instead of being angry and bitter, recognize that you're on the threshing floor. That's God working on you, to get rid of the unusable parts, the parts that are holding you back—the pride, the anger, the impatience. Now do your part and be willing to change, be pliable, be moldable. You may not like it, but if you keep the right attitude, it's refining you. You're going to come out better.

This is exactly what Peter did. Even though he had inconsistencies, even though at one moment he was defending Christ and the next moment he was denying Him, because he was pliable, because he kept growing, the old Peter didn't keep him from his destiny. It rose up from time to time, but Peter kept putting it back down and became the rock of the early church. You may

> *Draw a line and say, "This is a new day. I'm not letting the flesh rule me anymore. I'm done taking the easy way out. I'm going to be disciplined and keep the old man down."*

have let the old you get up more than you should. Be encouraged today. It's not going to keep you from your destiny. Draw a line and say, "This is a new day. I'm not letting the flesh rule me anymore. I'm done taking the easy way out. I'm going to be disciplined and keep the old man down." When you do this, bondages that have held you back will be broken, and you're going to step into a new season of freedom, a new season of growth, a new season of favor. Like Peter, you will overcome obstacles and become all you were created to be.

CHAPTER SIX

Stand Strong as God's Masterpiece

You are not what your environment says, not what your circumstances say, not what your feelings say, not what your thoughts say, but what God says.

We all face situations that challenge who God made us to be. He's put dreams in our heart, we're standing on His promises, knowing that we're blessed, strong, healthy, favored, but sometimes the circumstances say just the opposite. It's easy to let our environment change our identity. We know God calls us uniquely created, valuable, fearfully and wonderfully made. But when we go through unfair situations, when we're not treated right, when people walk away, we can lose who we are. We let those circumstances change how we see ourselves. Now we feel inferior, not attractive, nothing special. We're losing our true identity by adapting to the environment. We know we're a difference maker, we are well able, but doors haven't opened, the dream didn't work out, nobody supported us. Now instead of seeing ourselves as victorious and successful, we let the environment determine our identity. We see ourselves as limited, at a disadvantage, with too many disappointments. Here's the key: Your environment doesn't change who God created you to be. God says you're blessed, you're

> *Your environment doesn't change who God created you to be.*

favored, you're healthy. Everything around you may say just the opposite. This is what faith is all about. You have to dig down deep and say, "I am not going to let my environment define who I am. I am who God says I am."

"Joel, I thought I'd be further along. I thought I'd be in management by now, but I'm still stuck in the background. I thought I would have met someone, but I'm still single. I thought I'd be free from this illness, but I'm still dealing with it. I guess I'll always struggle." No, don't take that as your identity. Where you are is not who you are. The environment can change. One touch of God's favor can turn things around. The real question is, are you letting the environment change you? Are you taking on the identity of what's around you? The enemy would love for you to lose who you really are. He wants you to see yourself as limited, not attractive, a victim. That wrong identity will keep you from becoming who you were created to be.

You may be in an environment now that contradicts what God promised you. The circumstances look just the opposite of the dream He put in your heart. That's a test. You can adapt to the environment, water down your dream, and let it change you, or you can say, "No thanks. My environment doesn't dictate my identity. I know who I am. I am blessed. I am valuable. I am strong. I am victorious. I am a child of the Most High God."

YOU ARE NOT DEFINED BY YOUR ENVIRONMENT

Keep building up your mind and know you are a blessed child of God. Remember this as you work to build yourself up. Keep celebrating your God-given value by getting your mind going in the right direction. Standing strong as God's special creation will help you rediscover the forgotten you and reclaim the life you were created to live.

This is what Joseph had to do. He was seventeen years old when God gave him a dream that he would be a leader. He knew he was going to do great things. He shared his dream with his brothers, but they were already jealous of him because he was their father's favorite son. It only caused them to hate him even more. The brothers had gone to graze their father's flocks in pastures away from their home. After a few weeks, Joseph's father was concerned and sent Joseph to check on them. When they saw Joseph coming, they thought this was their big chance to get rid of him. They threw him into a pit where they were going to leave him to die, then they saw a caravan of Ishmaelite traders coming. So instead of letting Joseph die, they sold him as a slave into Egypt. He worked for a high ranking military officer, running all the affairs of his house, cleaning the rooms, maintaining the garden, doing repairs.

Joseph had the prophecy spoken over his life, the dream that he would lead a nation, but the environment contradicted what God promised him. The circumstances were the opposite of what Joseph saw in the dream. He was not leading; he was a slave. He was not telling people what to do; he was in captivity in a foreign country, with no freedom. He could have gotten bitter, seen himself as a victim, and said, "God, I don't understand." But you never read that Joseph complained or slacked off. He didn't let the environment change his identity. He kept seeing himself as who God said he would be: as a leader, as a difference maker.

> *When you face difficulties, things that are not fair, the enemy is not just trying to hinder your destiny, he's trying to steal your identity.*

When you face difficulties, things that are not

fair, the enemy is not just trying to hinder your destiny, he's trying to steal your identity. He's trying to deceive you into letting your environment dictate who you are through how people treat you, the disappointments you suffer, and delays you experience. If circumstances cause you to see yourself the wrong way, as limited, not valuable, and unworthy, that will keep you from your purpose. He's not after your possessions; he's after your identity. If he can control how you see yourself, he'll limit your future. When you're in a negative environment, do as Joseph did and don't let the environment get in you. You're not defined by your environment. Sometimes God is leading you into difficulties, allowing situations where people do you wrong. You know God has spoken to you and given a great dream for your life, but you find yourself in a pit. How you see yourself in the pit will determine whether you stay in that pit or whether you come out better. God wouldn't allow it if He wasn't going to use it to move you into greater levels of your destiny. In that pit, don't take on a victim mentality. Don't let

> *How you see yourself in the pit will determine whether you stay in that pit or whether you come out better.*

that bad break change your identity. You are a victor. You are an overcomer. You are more than a conqueror. You can do all things through Christ.

DON'T TAKE ON THE WRONG IDENTITY

Here's the key: The pit didn't change who you are. The environment didn't stop God's purpose for your life. Joseph was called to be the prince of Egypt. The fact is, he was a prince in a pit. That pit didn't change his calling. He was later put in prison for something he didn't do. He could have lost his identity and thought, *Man, I'll never lead a nation now. I'm not only a slave, I'm a prisoner.* No, the environment didn't dictate his identity. He was a prince in prison. He knew he was who God said he was whether he was in the pit, the prison, or the palace. You may be in circumstances you don't understand that could make you feel like a victim—the medical report is not good, people have done you wrong, a door closed on your dream. Can I tell you that you're a prince in the prison, you're a prince in the pit, and the good news is, you're going to be a prince in the palace.

Stand Strong as God's Masterpiece

Your time is coming. What God promised you, He will still bring to pass.

When Pharaoh, the leader of the nation, had a dream he didn't understand, he was told that a prisoner named Joseph could interpret dreams. The Scripture says, "Joseph was brought quickly to the palace." God knows how to suddenly turn things around. He interpreted Pharaoh's dream, and Pharaoh made Joseph second-in-command of the whole nation. He became the prince of Egypt. But look at all the opportunities Joseph had to lose his identity. He was lied about, betrayed, mistreated, and when Pharaoh's imprisoned butler, whose dream Joseph had interpreted, got out of prison, he forgot all about Joseph. If he had let his environment determine who he was, we wouldn't be talking about him. Like Joseph, we all have opportunities to lose who we really are. You go through a breakup, a divorce, and thoughts will start telling you, *You're not valuable, you're not attractive, and nobody wants to be around you.* Don't take on that defeated identity. That's not who you are. You're made in the image

> "My God determines my identity. I am who God says I am."

of God. You have royal blood flowing through your veins. God has crowned you with His favor. People don't determine who you are. They don't decide your worth and value. When your circumstances are saying just the opposite, you have to do as Joseph did and say, "No, this pit didn't change who I am; I'm a prince in the pit. This prison didn't lessen my value; I'm a prince in the prison. My circumstances don't determine my identity; my God determines my identity. I am who God says I am."

Sometimes you can take on the wrong identity. You've let what happened to you, what someone said, mistakes you've made, or how you were raised to cause you to feel like a victim, like you're not valuable. You used to have passion, believe for big things, but doors have closed. You went through setbacks. Now you've lost who you are. You've accepted a season or a moment in your story as being the full story; you've let go of the true you to whom God has instilled talent, favor, and great promise.

> *Nothing that's happened to you—the disappointments, the betrayals, the mistakes—have changed what God promised.*

It's important to lift up your head, stop looking at

what's around you, and remember who God is and what He has promised you. We tend to only see part of the story. We focus on the moment, but God sees the whole story. He will lead us step by step if we just follow Him. That truth can help you when you are down in the pit. You need to shake off all those lies, break all those strongholds, and start to practice seeing yourself as God sees you. You're a history maker. You're a barrier breaker. You are valuable. The dream God put in your heart is still on the way. Nothing that's happened to you—the disappointments, the betrayals, the mistakes—have changed what God promised. You're still a prince. You're still victorious. You're still favored. You're still going to become who He created you to be.

SEE YOURSELF AS GOD SEES YOU

From the time Jim was five years old, he had a terrible problem with stuttering. Other kids at school laughed and made fun of him. He became very insecure, isolated himself, wouldn't talk with others or go play with friends. He didn't want to be ridiculed. He loved to write poetry. When other kids were out playing sports, he stayed inside and focused on his poems. When he was a teenager, one of his teachers loved poetry too. Finding out that Jim was a gifted writer, she tried to get him to read his poems in the classroom, but he wasn't about to. When he was nervous, he stuttered too badly and could hardly get one word out.

One day this teacher came up with a plan. When Jim turned in a brilliant writing assignment, she said in front of the whole class, "Jim, I don't think you wrote this poem. There's no way. This is so good."

He responded through a stutter, "No, ma'am. I did write it."

She said, "I don't believe you. I've been teaching for years and never seen anything close to being this good."

He said it again, more stuttering, but more emphatically, "I promise you that I wrote it."

"Then you're going to have to prove it to me," she said. "You have to read it in front of the class so I can see that you know it."

Jim reluctantly walked up to the front. Gripping the paper, his hands were shaking. Some of the kids were snickering, whispering to one another, "Here comes the stuttering!" But when he began to read the poem, the rhythm of what he wrote flowed out so naturally that he never stuttered a word. He couldn't believe it, the kids couldn't believe it, and the teacher was in awe.

As he continued reading, they also discovered that he had an amazing voice, deep, resonant, compelling. He read his own words with incredible passion and skill.

From that time on, Jim never stuttered again. Today, we know Jim as James Earl Jones, who passed away in 2024. Not only did he become a great actor known for roles in film, television, and theater but he was the iconic voice of Darth Vader in *Star Wars* and Mufasa in *The Lion King*.

I believe that down deep you know God has put great things in you. You know you can rise higher, you can set a new standard for your family, you can teach the class, you can beat the sickness, you can break the addiction. But maybe like Jim, you're stuck, letting fear, guilt, shame, intimidation, and weaknesses convince you to live hiding your gifts, hiding what God put in you. If you see yourself as lacking, at a disadvantage, or unworthy, it is limiting your life. It's not that you don't have great potential; it may be that your self-image has been so damaged and distorted over the years that you've forgotten the real you. It's as though you're in a room filled with distorting mirrors at the carnival and none of the images you see are true images. It's not who you really are. Like Jim's teacher, I want to help you get rid of the distorting mirror with its wrong images and rediscover the real you.

YOUR STORY IS NOT OVER

I know another young woman who was raised in a limited environment. She also came from a dysfunctional family. Her father was never around, and her mother had addictions. The poverty, defeat, and compromise she experienced as a child had become her identity. She didn't know any better. She saw herself as limited, not talented, not valuable. We often adapt to the environment and don't even realize it. It's what we've seen modeled growing up. It's how our friends and neighbors live. That becomes how we see ourselves. At sixteen years old, this young lady got pregnant and had to drop out of school. It looked as though the negative family cycle would continue. She was on welfare, living in government housing, raising her son, with no future to speak of. One day someone invited her to Lakewood. She started attending week after week. She would hear me talk about how you have seeds of greatness, how you were created to live a victorious life, and when you see yourself as God sees you, you can break barriers of the past and rise to new levels. As she started to reprogram her thinking, she began to accept her true identity. Instead of letting her environment dictate who she was, she started believing she was who God said she was—blessed, talented, confident, valuable, with a bright future.

> When you see yourself as God sees you, you can break barriers of the past and rise to new levels.

She got a job at the school cafeteria, cleaning dishes, making minimum wage. While she was grateful, something inside was saying she was made for more. She could feel her destiny calling her. She didn't settle for the status quo. She went back to school and got her GED. She wasn't satisfied and decided to go to college. She would work during the day and go to school at night. In four years, she graduated with honors. She still wasn't satisfied and went back to school and got her master's degree. Today she's the principal at the same school where she used to work in the cafeteria.

Don't let your environment dictate your identity. The truth is that this woman was a principal when she was washing dishes. She was a leader when she was a child in her dysfunctional home. She just didn't know it. On the way to your destiny, there will be environments that contradict what God has for you. It's tempting to let what's not happening define who you are. "I guess I'll always be lonely. I'll never get healthy again. I'll never be successful." Those circumstances don't define you. As with this young woman, there are things in you that you haven't discovered. Your story is not yet complete. Pharaoh is going to call. The doors are going to open. What God promised you is still on schedule.

Don't get talked out of who you know you are. You may get thrown into a pit, but you have to remind yourself, "This pit didn't change who I am. I'm a prince in the pit, I'm a prince in the prison, and I'm a prince in the palace." The question is, will you keep your identity as you pass through the pit and through the prison? Will you not let the environment convince you that you must have heard God wrong? "The opposition is too

> *Will you keep your identity as you pass through the pit and through the prison?*

big. I'm not that talented. I can't reach my dreams. It would have happened by now." Tune out those lies and keep your mind on what God says about you. "I'm blessed. I'm talented. My future is bright. God is breathing in my direction. I will become all I was created to be."

WHERE YOU ARE IS NOT WHO YOU ARE

Think about David. The prophet Samuel came to his father's house to choose the next king of Israel. Samuel saw David's seven older brothers, but he passed over them and chose David, the least likely one. It was an amazing moment. David's brothers were bigger, stronger, and more experienced, but Samuel poured the oil on David and anointed him to be the next king. What's interesting is that David didn't go right to the palace; he went back to the shepherds' fields. He was out there tending sheep week after week, month after month. He knew he was a king. He felt the oil running down his head. He heard the prophet declare it, but his circumstances said just the opposite. He was still out taking care of sheep, shoveling the waste, gathering their food. I can imagine him at night, alone, no one to talk to, and thinking, *Maybe I'm not a king. Maybe Samuel was wrong. If I was going to do great things, why am I still stuck out here?* The enemy knows if he can steal your identity by convincing you that you're not who God says you are, he can keep you from your destiny.

David's environment didn't line up with the prophecy spoken over him. He had no one to lead, no one that looked up to him, no influence. But David understood this principle: "My environment doesn't define who I am. God defines who I am. God says I'm a king, so I'm going to have a king mentality." David led those sheep with excellence. He used his sling to protect the animals like he was protecting God's people. Others passing by wouldn't have paid any attention. "There's that shepherd boy. No big deal." What they didn't know was he was a king in the shepherds' fields. His time was coming. One day he defeated Goliath, and he was thrust into influence and favor that he had never seen. He became who God said he was. Don't let your environment talk you out

> *Don't lose your identity over something that's going to change.*

of what God promised you. Keep seeing yourself as a king even though you're in the shepherds' fields right now. That's just a season. Your story isn't over. Keep seeing yourself as a principal even though you're washing dishes. See yourself as a prince even though you're in the pit. Where you are is not who you are. Don't get bitter over a temporary season. Don't lose your identity over something that's going to change.

This is where some people miss God's best. They get discouraged and allow it to change who they are. "I'll never step into leadership, never expand my business, never see my family restored. I'm in a pit." You're right where Joseph was. "I'm stuck at this same position." You're right where David was. "I was raised in dysfunction. I've had a lot of bad breaks." You're right where that young woman was. You're letting a temporary season, something that contradicts what God put in you, to change who you are. It's time to dig down deep, remember who you are, and remember what God has promised you. It's time to say, "I'm not moved by the circumstances. I'm not bitter over the delay. I'm not upset with my brothers who threw me into a pit. None of these things are going to change who I know God made me to be."

CIRCUMSTANCES DO NOT DICTATE YOUR IDENTITY

A friend of mine told me that when he was six years old, his teacher gave the class an assignment. They had to write down what they wanted to be when they grew up. He had seen a man on television who was very funny. That was his dream. As a little boy, he knew he wanted to be on television making people laugh. He wrote it down. He came from a low-income family. They didn't have much, plus he had a stuttering problem. The teacher started calling the kids' names out and reading what they had written. When she came to his, she stopped and said, "Little Stevie, please come up here." He started walking to the front of the class so proud, thinking she was going to congratulate him, but it was just the opposite. She said, "Stevie, what did you write?" He said, "I wrote that I want to be on television making people laugh." She asked, "Now, Stevie, do you know anyone on television?" He responded, "No, ma'am." She said, "Has anyone in your family ever been on television?" He said, "No, ma'am." She said, "Then you take this back and write down something more realistic."

As a little six-year-old boy, he was confused.

Nobody had ever told him what he couldn't become. That night he told his father what happened. He showed him the paper where he had written that he wanted to be on television. His father said, "Listen here, Stevie. You put this in your top drawer, and every morning before you go to school and every night before you go to bed, you look at that paper and thank God that one day you will be on television." This little boy had no money, no connections, no way in the natural, but God is supernatural. He won't put a dream in your heart that He can't bring to pass. But there will be times of testing, when circumstances seem just the opposite. People will tell you, "It's not going to happen. Don't get your hopes up." Let that go in one ear and out the other. People don't determine your destiny. They can't see what God put in you. They didn't hear what God whispered to you in the night. Don't expect everyone to cheer you on.

David's own father didn't even call him in from the shepherds' fields when Samuel first came to the house. Don't be surprised if the environment, the people around you, contradict what God has spoken to you. That doesn't mean it's not going to happen. That's a sign that it's on the way. Your part is to not let it change how you see yourself. Come into agreement with what God has spoken over your life. Get your identity from Him and not from people, not from circumstances, not from feelings. If you're relying on those things, you'll take on the wrong identity.

This little boy grew up with the dream God put in his heart. All the circumstances said it would never happen. In his late twenties, for three years he was homeless, living out of his car. His environment said, "You'll never get out of this pit." But deep down, like Joseph, he knew he was a prince in a pit. He knew that the favor of God was on his life. He kept seeing himself as successful, lifting people up, making a difference with his life. God began to open doors and bring the right people. Today that young boy Stevie is Steve Harvey. He's on television all the time, making people laugh. He gives all the credit to God. Are you letting your environment define who you are? Are your circumstances dictating your identity? You need to go back to who God says you are. That's where you'll find the forgotten you—still whole, still chosen, and still equipped to live out the life God designed for you. Don't let the negative circumstances talk you out of what God has spoken over your life.

TAKE YOUR PROMISED LAND

When Moses sent twelve spies into the Promised Land, ten spies came back after forty days and said, "Moses, we don't have a chance. The people are huge. We felt like grasshoppers compared to them." Notice how they saw themselves. Of all the analogies they could have come up with, they used a little insect that hops around. They could have at least said, "We're like a gerbil. We're like a rabbit." I'll take a goat over a grasshopper. What's amazing is these ten spies were the cream of the crop. They were warriors. They were leaders, skilled and strong. On top of that, they had seen God part the Red Sea, bring water out of a rock, send manna each morning. But they made the mistake of letting their environment determine their identity. Because they saw themselves as grasshoppers, as weak, defeated, and "not able to," they never did go into the Promised Land.

Don't let that be you. What you're up against may look impossible. It's easy to take on a grasshopper mentality and water down your dreams. On your own, you may not be able to defeat it, but you're not on your own. The Most High God is breathing on your life. At the appointed time, Pharaoh will call you. At the appointed time, the giant will fall, the door will open, the healing will come, the child will turn around. Your circumstances may look just the opposite, but you're right where you're supposed to be. The environment is trying to convince you to change who you are. Don't fall into that trap. You are blessed. You are favored. You are healthy. You are valuable. You are strong. You are victorious. Like Joseph, you're coming out of any pit, any defeat, any sickness, any addiction, and you're going into the palace, into freedom, into abundance, into wholeness. Like David, you're coming out of any shepherds' fields into leadership, influence, resources, and abundance. Get ready. Strongholds are coming down, and new doors are opening.

> *Like Joseph, you're coming out of any pit, any defeat, any sickness, any addiction, and you're going into the palace, into freedom, into abundance, into wholeness.*

CHAPTER SEVEN

Know That You Are Destined for Greatness

God put greatness in you, a person of destiny in you, a mighty hero in you, and there's a calling on your life, a purpose for you to accomplish.

When I was twenty years old, I went to India with my father. It was my first time being overseas. One evening I was sitting on the beach by myself watching the sunset. It was so beautiful, almost surreal. There were miles of pure white sand, swaying palm trees, and glistening blue water. The sun was huge on the horizon, just about to set. I remember the distinct smells, the saltwater from the ocean spray, the smoke from the people who were grilling on the beach, and the marijuana from the hippies who were getting high! It looked like a postcard. I had never seen anything so magnificent. It made me think about how God is such an amazing painter, such an amazing artist.

As I was sitting there reflecting on my life, I heard God ask me, not out loud, just an impression in my spirit, "Joel, you think this is a beautiful picture, don't you?" I said, "Yes, God. It's a magnificent picture." He asked, "What do you think My most prized painting would be, My most incredible creation?" I thought

> *"What do you think My most prized painting would be, My most incredible creation?"*

about it a moment and said, "God, it must be this. This is beautiful." He said, "No, it's not this sunset." Earlier that year I had been in the Rocky Mountains, which were so beautiful. I said, "I bet it's the Rocky Mountains." He responded, "No, it's not that." I thought, *What could it be? The Grand Canyon, the solar system, the Milky Way?* He said, "No, Joel. My most prized creation, the one I'm the most proud of, is you." I thought, *Me? It can't be me. I'm just average. There's nothing special about me.* He continued, "Joel, you don't understand. When I made the solar system, the sun, oceans, and mountains, that was all good. I'm proud of that. But when I made you, I breathed My life into you. I created you in My own image. I put My spiritual DNA in you. You are My special creation."

THE PROMISE IS TO YOU, NOT TO SOMEONE ELSE

We learn in Judges 6 that powerful tribes of desert nomads called the Midianites and Amalekites had controlled the people of Israel for seven years, invading the land, ruining the crops and taking their herds. There was a young man named Gideon who was threshing wheat in a winepress, hidden from view. He was afraid and intimidated. He had seen how vast and powerful the enemy was, their skill and expertise. He knew that his people didn't have a chance against them. While he was hiding, an angel came into the winepress and said, "Mighty hero, the Lord is with you." I can imagine Gideon looked around, thinking, *Who are you talking to? I'm not a mighty hero. I'm afraid. I'm hiding.*

Gideon responded, "How can I rescue Israel? I come from the smallest tribe, and I'm the least one in my family." Here God had just called him a mighty hero. Gideon's perception of who he was, inadequate and insecure, was keeping him from becoming who God called him to be. But Gideon finally changed his thinking. He got a new image of who he was, and he went out and defeated the Midianites. He saved the people of Israel. But when he was sitting in that winepress, feeling afraid and inferior, he never dreamed we would be talking about him today. He never dreamed he would become a hero of faith. If the angel had not shown up to speak to his destiny, to tell him who God created him to be, he would have lived and died and never discovered who he really was. Maybe God sent me, like that angel, to tell you who you really are. You're not what people say you

> *You're not what people say you are. You're not limited by how you were raised. You're not what your feelings say you are.*

are. You're not limited by how you were raised. You're not what your feelings say you are. Your feelings don't always tell the truth. You may feel weak, insecure, not valuable, not qualified, but don't let your feelings determine your identity. Feelings are fickle. Feelings will come and go. You have to go back to what your Creator says. He calls you a mighty hero. He calls you a barrier breaker, a giant killer, a masterpiece, a prized possession.

I can imagine that as Gideon was threshing wheat in the winepress, he had been praying for God to send a great leader, believing for the right person to show up. "God, send us a deliverer. Send us someone strong, talented, with Your favor, with Your blessing." He didn't realize that he was the one he was praying for. He was the answer he was asking God for. I

> *When we're always looking to others, always counting on someone else, it's because we're overlooking what God put in us.*

wonder if, like Gideon, you're the one you've been praying for. You're the one to do great things, to set a new standard, to take your family to a new level. When we're always looking to others, always counting on someone else, it's because we're overlooking what God put in us. Don't overlook yourself. Don't discount who you are, thinking everyone else is talented. No, God has destined you to do something awesome, something that only you can accomplish. When you remember you're destined for greatness, something powerful happens—you awaken the greatness God placed inside you. That truth will stir your passion, reignite your dreams, and lead you into the abundant life you were created to enjoy.

In the previous chapter, I described how Abraham and Sarah were way too old to have a baby, yet God gave them His promise. Years went by, with no sign of a child. So, Sarah told Abraham to sleep with her maid, Hagar, thinking that this was the way they could have a baby. Hagar had a child through Abraham, Ishmael, but he wasn't the promised child. God said to Sarah, "I didn't put the promise in someone else. I put the promise in you." Sarah was discounting herself. "I'm too old. There's no way. I can't have a baby at my age." As long as she saw herself as barren, not able to have children, she was limiting her destiny. She had to start seeing herself as a mother, seeing that baby in her arms. When she changed her perception of who she was, when she quit counting on other people to make it happen, she believed and said, "I'm the one to give birth to this child." That's when she conceived and gave birth to baby Isaac at ninety years old.

God will put promises in your heart that seem impossible. Thoughts will tell you all the reasons it's not going to happen. If you look at it only in the natural, you'll talk yourself out of it. How do you know you're not a Sarah, that God is going to do something out of the ordinary, something uncommon? How do you know you're not a Gideon, a mighty hero, someone who will take your family where you've never been? It's easy to think, *That's not who I am. That's for someone younger, more talented, more influential, more attractive.* No, God put the promise in you, not someone else. You've been raised up for such a time as this. Don't discount who you are. It's good

> *How do you know you're not a Sarah, that God is going to do something out of the ordinary, something uncommon?*

to celebrate others, but you need to recognize that you're gifted, you're talented, you're valuable, you're fearfully and wonderfully made.

YOU ARE THE ANSWER TO YOUR OWN PRAYER

There was a poor little boy named Todd Price growing up in rural Kentucky. When he was eight years old, he heard that he could support a hungry child in a foreign country for fifteen dollars a month, which sounded like a lot when you have no money. But he had an intense desire to try to help, so he did what he could and started mowing lawns and was able to support one child. He continued to increase his giving through high school and college, then on to medical school and the opening of his own medical practice as an infectious disease specialist. All the while, he did whatever he could, taking overseas trips with doctors to help take care of children. When one of his medical suppliers heard about what he was doing, they asked if they could help out and began donating skid loads of medicines and other supplies. Then another donor sent him thousands of pairs of shoes to protect children from infections and parasitic diseases. The same happened with hospital beds that were being replaced in one hospital. This all began a practice of Dr. Todd Price and his wife, Sue, receiving and placing around a billion dollars' worth of medication and medical supplies to local health partners in thirty-seven countries across the developing world. It's interesting that as a little boy, Todd always prayed that God would find someone who was rich to do what was on his heart. He told me, "Joel, I never realized I was the person I was praying for."

Sometimes, like Dr. Price and like Gideon, we don't recognize who we are. We have all this potential inside, these God-given dreams and abilities. But often our circumstances, other people, and our own thoughts tell us that we're ordinary, limited, and can't do anything significant. We go through life with little dreams, feeling unqualified, praying that someone else will make a difference; someone else will push our family forward. Here's the key: You're the one you're praying for. There are doors God will open that you could never imagine in your wildest dreams. You may not see how it can happen. That's okay. That's when God steps in. He'll breathe in your direction and give you favor, ability, and blessings that take you where you can't go on your own.

Know That You Are Destined for Greatness

It's significant that the angel said to Gideon, "Mighty hero, the Lord is with you." He could have just said, "Gideon, God wants you to go deliver the Israelites." God knew He had to convince Gideon to see himself as He saw him. He had to help him discover who he really was, a mighty hero. As long as he saw himself as weak, limited, and from the wrong family, I wouldn't be writing about him. Don't miss your destiny because you don't recognize who you are.

When my father passed in 1999, God had to do the same for me. I felt His call to step up and pastor the church, but like Gideon, I heard the fear and insecurities telling me that I'd just make a fool of myself and no one would listen to me. I overheard people saying to one another, "He's not as good as his father. This church will never make it with Joel." All these voices were trying to push me down and limit my potential. There was a battle taking place in my mind over who I was going to be. Was I going to be what people said, what my doubts said, what my feelings said? I had to make the decision that Gideon made: *Am I going to sit here and let my fears and doubts talk me out of stepping up, or am I going to believe what God says about me? He says I'm strong in the Lord and I can do all things through Christ.* I

> *Once you think you know who you are, God will take you higher. He'll trust you with more.*

took that step of faith and never dreamed where God would take me. I thought I knew who I was, but I'm still discovering who I am. I've learned that once you think you know who you are, God will take you higher. He'll trust you with more. He's taking you from glory to glory.

A CHILD-OF-THE-KING MENTALITY

In the Scripture, there was a young boy named Mephibosheth. He was the grandson of King Saul and the son of Jonathan, David's best friend. He was born into royalty, destined to one day take the throne. But when he was five years old, his grandfather and father were killed in battle on the same day. After the enemy finished off King Saul, they headed into town to find Saul's family. When Mephibosheth's nurse heard the news, she picked him up and took off running as fast as she could, trying to spare his life. But as she fled, she dropped Mephibosheth, and he became crippled in both feet and would never walk again. He ended up living in hiding in a place called Lo Debar, one of the poorest, most run-down cities of that day. Here is the grandson of the king, raised in royalty in the palace, but now he's in the slums, barely surviving.

When we've been through disappointments, loss, and bad breaks, it's easy to forget who we are and let that become our identity. "I've been dropped. I've been hurt. I've been betrayed. I have a good excuse to be this way." But what you've been through didn't change who you are. You are still a child of the Most High God. He's promised to give you beauty for the ashes, to pay you back double for the unfair things. But you have to get your passion back, get your vision back. The enemy would love for the bad break to define you. But God saw what happened. He saw who left you. He saw what you didn't get. He's a God of justice. He's going to make it up to you.

> *The enemy would love for the bad break to define you.*

Years went by, and Mephibosheth was a grown man. One day King David was thinking about his good friend Jonathan, how much he loved and missed him. He asked his staff if any of King Saul's relatives were still alive. They said, "Yes, he has a grandson, but he's crippled." David said, "Bring him to me." The king's men showed up in the slums of Lo Debar. You can imagine the commotion; everyone was talking. "What are they doing here? Who are they looking for?" When they came and knocked on Mephibosheth's door, I'm sure his heart must have sunk as he saw the officials. I can imagine what was going through his mind as he scooted across the floor to answer the door. *Oh man, they found me. I'm in big trouble. My grandfather threw spears at David, tried to kill him, and chased him through the desert for years. David's about to get revenge. This is going to be the end.*

The main leader said to him, "Mephibosheth, the king is looking for you and wants us to bring you to him." They picked him up and carried him to the palace. When they brought Mephibosheth before David, the first thing he said was, "Why would you even bother with a dead dog like me?" He saw himself as not valuable, unworthy, a victim. "I don't deserve anything. Look what I've been through. I'm at a disadvantage." In reality, he was the grandson of the king, unique in all the world. He was royalty. Just because someone dropped him didn't change his name. He didn't suddenly not become King Saul's grandson. The problem was, he let life change his name. He let that bad break define his identity. He forgot who he was and the life God had called him to.

I can see him trembling with fear, so worried about what David was going to do to him. David said, in effect, "Mephibosheth, I'm not here to harm you. I'm here to remind you who you are. You're royalty. You're the grandson of the king. Your father was my best friend. From now on, you're going to live in the palace with me. Every night you will sit at my table and have dinner. All the land that belonged to your grandfather, I'm giving to you." I can see Mephibosheth wiping tears from his eyes. His face begins to brighten. He can't believe it. He said, "Do you mean I'm not a dead dog? I'm not unworthy? I'm not washed up?" David said, "No, that's not who you are. You don't belong in Lo Debar. You belong in the palace with me." I wonder how many of us,

> *I wonder how many of us, like Mephibosheth, have that dead-dog mentality, believing that our lives are broken and without any purpose.*

like Mephibosheth, have that dead-dog mentality, believing that our lives are broken and without any purpose. Can I tell you that the King is looking for you. Not for someone else, but for you. Now get rid of that dead-dog mentality and start having a child-of-the-King mentality. You are worthy, valuable, forgiven, blessed, abundant, victorious.

THE KING IS LOOKING FOR YOU

When my nephew Jackson was a little boy, just a toddler, my sister-in-law Jennifer, my brother Paul's wife, would take him to bed each night. After they prayed, she would go through a long list of superheroes, telling Jackson who he was, just to make him feel loved and valuable. She would say, "Jackson, you're my Superman, you're my Rescue Hero, you're my Buzz Lightyear, you're my Lightning McQueen, you're my Power Ranger," and on and on. He would lie there with a big smile and take it all in. One night they got home late. She put him to bed in a hurry and didn't go through the list. After a few minutes, she heard this voice calling loudly, "Momma! Momma!" She rushed to his room and said, "Jackson, what's wrong?" He said, "Mom, you forgot to tell me who I am."

Too many people have never been told who they are. They've had negative voices playing in their minds over and over, "You're average. You're not talented. You're unattractive. You're nothing special. You'll never do anything great," and they've believed the lies. No, let me tell you who you really are. You're a child of the Most High God. You're beautiful, you're talented, you're strong, you're successful, you're one of a kind, a history maker, a giant killer, a mighty hero.

The apostle Paul says in Romans 8, "The entire universe is standing on tiptoe, yearning to see the unveiling of God's glorious sons and daughters." He's saying that all of Heaven is waiting for you to recognize who you are and remember the gifts and talents that God put in you.

> *All of Heaven is waiting for you to recognize who you are.*

They're standing on tiptoe, thinking, *Maybe they'll get it today. Maybe they'll realize that they're gifted, a mighty hero, the King's son. Maybe today they'll realize they don't belong in Lo Debar, that they can step up to the table, that they're royalty.* If you want to give Heaven something to cheer about, see yourself the way God sees you. Quit discounting yourself, thinking you're at a disadvantage, you're lacking, not qualified. Get out of Lo Debar. Get out of that negative mindset and come over to the palace. The King is looking for you. Like Gideon, you're going to discover talent, courage, creativity, and favor you never knew you had. You will overcome obstacles that had seemed insurmountable, and accomplish more than you have ever dreamed possible.

CHAPTER EIGHT

Forget the Past, Focus on the Future

God has put an end to everything that is trying to keep you imprisoned by your past—the guilt, the hurts, the failures, the threats—and from stepping forward into the greatness He has for you.

We've all had negative experiences that could hold us back. We may have made mistakes at times, compromised and done things we shouldn't. We can end up living in regrets, feeling guilty, down on ourselves. Sometimes it's from what other people have done to us. Hurts, betrayals, or what they said have left scars and wounds that can taint our future and cause us to feel inferior and not worthy. Some people have gone through trauma and lived with dysfunction, a rough childhood, a toxic relationship. They take on a false sense of responsibility, thinking they're to blame. *I must not be good enough or they wouldn't have treated me that way.* It's easy to become imprisoned by our past to where we don't move forward. We have these skeletons in our closet. We live afraid and go into hiding. *What if someone finds out? There's going to be embarrassment and shame.*

Here's the good news: Nothing in your past has to stop your future. No failure you've made is too much for the mercy of

> *How much power are you giving to your past— the guilt, hurts, mistakes, threats?*

God. No hurt, no injustice, no trauma that you've been through has stopped what God has purposed for you. You can't live looking in the rearview mirror and reach your destiny. How much power are you giving to your past—the guilt, hurts, mistakes, threats?

When we've been through negative things, it's easy to develop a fear of it happening again. *Don't get in a new relationship. You'll just get hurt again. You can't be in leadership. You can't accomplish your dreams. You've made too many mistakes.* That's the enemy doing what he does best, trying to use your past to convince you to shrink back so you won't become who you were created to be. Don't believe those lies. Don't dwell on the past—leave it behind and set your eyes on the bright future God has in store. As you keep declaring His promises and standing on His Word, you'll rediscover the amazing person He created you to be, and you'll step into the destiny that's been waiting for you all along.

Before the apostle Paul wrote almost half the books in the New Testament, he was called Saul and was the biggest enemy of the early church. He hated and persecuted believers, constantly making threats,

Forget the Past, Focus on the Future

arresting them and putting them in prison, which led to many deaths. But in one moment on the road to Damascus, God changed his life. He went from being known as Saul to being the apostle Paul. Paul could have lived in regrets, thinking, *I can't do anything great. I can't lead believers whom people know I hated. I can't write books promoting Christ. I have too many skeletons in my closet. I've done too much harm.* If Paul had become imprisoned by his past, we would be missing much of the New Testament today. What will people miss out on if you let the past keep you from sharing your gifts? "Joel, I have too many skeletons in my closet too." No, when you asked God to forgive you, He cleaned your closet. You can move forward in faith. All those threats—*You're going to be embarrassed. You're not worthy. It's going to happen again*—have been taken care of. What's trying to harm you has already been defeated. That's just the enemy trying to keep you paralyzed by the past. Break out of that box and step into the greatness God has for you.

> **What will people miss out on if you let the past keep you from sharing your gifts?**

BREAK GENERATIONAL LIMITATIONS

In the Scripture, Nimrod was the great-grandson of Noah. He had heard all about the huge flood that had covered the Earth, and how his great-grandfather and seven of his relatives were the only ones spared. It was such a traumatic event that even though he lived two generations later, it had a major impact on him. He was afraid that it might happen again. He lived in fear, worried, traumatized by an event that his relatives went through. Studies show how trauma can be passed down, how things your ancestors dealt with even before you were born can affect the expression of your DNA. Research studies show that effects upon the survivors of the extreme trauma of the Holocaust can be found in their children and grandchildren, that later generations still experienced the fears and threats and triggers. Even though they were completely safe, even though it was all behind them, they still had to deal with the feelings, the thoughts, the imaginations. It wasn't as though they were being weak and could be told, "Come on, get over it." There were real issues, and not just mental, but biological. The generational trauma became a part of their psychology and even their biology.

Forget the Past, Focus on the Future

You may wonder why you have to deal with certain tendencies, such as low self-esteem, or that you can't trust people in a relationship, or you're afraid someone is going to leave, or why you are always thinking that nothing good will happen. Perhaps you have something like a spirit of oppression that makes you want to shrink back. Those can be traits that might have been passed down. But here's the key: God has raised you up to break them. You're the one to put a stop to generational limitations and to start generational blessings. Just as trauma, dysfunction, and wounds from hurts can be passed down, so can blessings, favor, confidence, integrity, and victory. You don't have to let the past dictate your future. You can break free and set a new standard.

> *You don't have to let the past dictate your future. You can break free and set a new standard.*

Genesis 11 tells the story of the Tower of Babel. While not directly stated in Scripture, it is believed that Nimrod was its builder. The tower was intended to be like a huge skyscraper, reaching up to the heavens. Many Jewish scholars believe that one of the reasons Nimrod built this tower was to have a high place to go in case it flooded again. He was building this structure out of fear, so he could escape what could be coming. He didn't have a big boat like his great-grandfather, but he had a tower. He either didn't realize God had promised the Earth would never flood again or he didn't believe it. He'd heard all about the water, but he hadn't believed the message of the rainbow. How many things are we planning out of fear of what's happened in the past? We're doing what Nimrod did. We're building up walls and defenses based on negative things of the past.

> *How many things are we planning out of fear of what's happened in the past?*

It's interesting that construction on the Tower of Babel was halted and abandoned. God intervened and confused the language of the builders, and then scattered them across the Earth. They couldn't finish it. We've all been through floods, had hurts, and made mistakes. There may be negative things that have been passed down. But God is showing us that we don't have to live in fear of the past. *What if it happens again? I better shrink back, put up walls, and make plans for defeat.* No, don't be a Nimrod. Don't spend your life fearing the past, paralyzed by what might happen. You can't step into your future if you're stuck in the past, building towers, trying to escape the next flood, afraid of what could happen. When the fear of your past tries to hold you back, tries to get you discouraged and worried, look up in the sky. By faith, see that rainbow. God is saying, "It's not going to flood again. I've taken care of your past. I've cleaned your closets. I've forgiven your mistakes. I've planned beauty for the ashes, joy for the mourning, healing for the hurts, and new beginnings for the loss." Don't waste your time building a Tower of Babel, making plans to escape the hurts, escape the trauma, escape the flood. If you're going to build anything, build a tower of hope, a tower of faith. Believe that your past is forgiven, that the threats are gone, that what's held you back has been broken, and that you are free to step into the favor and blessing and joy that God has destined for you.

THE PAST WILL COME CHASING

When the Israelites were delivered out of slavery, they left Egypt and headed toward the Promised Land. After years of abuse and mistreatment, these two million people were finally free. I can hear them singing and see them giving high fives as they were leaving, so excited. But then Pharaoh changed his mind and sent his army chasing after them. Pharaoh represents the past—the hurts, the trauma, the mistakes, the injustice. The past will always come chasing you. The Israelites were trying to move forward into their future; they knew God had opened this door but they couldn't escape the past. Pharaoh's army was catching up. They could hear the hoofbeats from the horses getting closer and closer. Anytime you try to move forward, don't be surprised if you hear the past chasing you, reminding you of the mistakes you've made. "You can't expect anything good. You don't deserve it. The hurts and the wrongs will happen again. People will walk away." Those are the hoofbeats. That's the enemy whispering lies, trying to get you paralyzed by your past.

The Israelites came to a dead end at the Red Sea. Their past caught up to them. Pharaoh and all the

> *Anytime you try to move forward, don't be surprised if you hear the past chasing you, reminding you of the mistakes you've made.*

Forget the Past, Focus on the Future

chariots were just a few miles back. It looked as though the people would be recaptured and taken back to Egypt. But God will never let your past dictate your future. He will always make a way of escape. You may hear the hoofbeats of your past chasing you now. You try to move forward, but there's always that guilt, that fear, the nagging feeling that you're going to be hurt again, that the past mistake will always haunt you. You can't seem to get away from your past. That's what happened to the Israelites. They had nowhere to go, then suddenly the Red Sea parted. God made a way where they didn't see a way. Those two million people went through on dry ground.

That could have been the end of the story. The waters closed up and kept Pharaoh's army on the other side. That would have been a great miracle. But God knew the Israelites would always be looking over their shoulders, living in fear, expecting that Pharaoh's army might show up at any minute. God didn't want them to be focused on the past, living with that threat, wondering what might happen. So, He let the Red Sea stay open, and Pharaoh's army came chasing full speed ahead. I'm sure the Israelites thought, *They're still going to catch us. We made it through, but they're faster than us.* Right on cue, the walls of water came crashing down, and all the enemy drowned. None of them survived. Now the Israelites never had to fear Pharaoh again. The threat was gone.

Maybe you've had some hoofbeats chasing you. Every time you try to move ahead, you hear the past coming, reminding you of all your mistakes, all the threats, the hurts, what's never going to work out. Like God did for them, He's taken care of your past. You don't have to live looking over your shoulder, letting those hoofbeats cause you to shrink back and try to build a tower in case it happens again. This is a new day. That threat has been taken care of. Stop looking behind you; you can't move forward if you're looking back. Turn off all those images and start seeing yourself blessed, happy, in great relationships, accomplishing your dreams, and rising to new levels.

YOU ARE PREPARED BY YOUR PAST

The enemy wanted the Israelites to see themselves as runaway slaves. "You got free, but you're still a slave. You're still inferior, at a disadvantage. You're still going to be mistreated, face injustice, and have to struggle through life." He would love for the negative things in your past to determine your identity—how you see yourself, your value, your worth. If you've been mistreated, he'll whisper, "You're not valuable." If someone walked out on you and broke your heart, he'll say, "You're not attractive." If you've made mistakes and gotten off course, he declares, "You're not worthy. You can't be blessed. Your past has tainted your future." Don't believe those lies. Nothing that's happened in your past has lessened your value. You are still a son or daughter of the Most High God. You are still a masterpiece, one of a kind, a prized possession. Nothing you've been through—no trauma, no hurt, no injustice—has stopped the purpose God has for you. Nothing has canceled your assignment.

You are not defined by your past; you are prepared by your past. If God allowed something negative to happen, it deposited something in you that you're going to need for your future. Your job is to keep moving forward, making plans for the good things that are

> *If God allowed something negative to happen, it deposited something in you that you're going to need for your future.*

in store. The past that's been chasing you is buried in the Red Sea. God has taken care of that threat. Now move on toward your Promised Land.

GOD HAS TAKEN CARE OF YOUR PAST

When Moses was a young man, he knew he was supposed to deliver the Israelites out of Egyptian slavery. He was born a Hebrew slave but was raised in the palace by Pharaoh's daughter. One day he saw an Egyptian foreman mistreating a Hebrew slave. When he didn't think anyone was watching, he killed the foreman, thinking he was standing up for the Hebrews. You can do the right thing at the wrong time, and it's a mistake. Someone saw what Moses did, and he had to flee for his life. He spent years hiding in the desert, running from a mistake, running from his past. I'm sure he felt guilty, was down on himself, thinking he had missed his destiny. For forty years he hid his gifts, hid his talents, hid his dreams. Anytime he tried to move forward, there was the past telling him, "Look what you've done. You don't deserve to be blessed. You blew it." Sure, there are consequences for bad choices. He

Forget the Past, Focus on the Future

had to take a detour into the desert, but mistakes don't cancel your destiny. God doesn't write you off because you're not where you're supposed to be. He's going to give you another chance to do what He's called you to do.

After forty years, God showed up in a burning bush and said, "Moses, your time has come. Go tell Pharaoh to let My people go." I'm sure Moses thought, *No thanks, God. I'm not going back there. They know what I did. I'll get arrested, put in prison, and maybe killed.* He was saying to himself, "I have skeletons in my closet. I need to stay safe in hiding so no one will find out." Moses had all these reasons for why he couldn't do it and how he had been through too much and had too many people against him. But God has a way of cleaning your closets. You don't have to live haunted by your past, afraid to move forward. His mercy will cover your mistakes. God said in Exodus 4, "Moses, do not be afraid to return to Egypt, for all those who were trying to kill you are dead." Moses was living afraid of what might happen, hiding from his mistakes. God showed up and said, "I've already taken care of your past. I've put a stop to all the things that could have harmed you."

Are you doing like Moses, running from your

past, hiding because of mistakes, living in regrets? God is saying to you what He said to Moses, "Don't be afraid. I have taken care of your past." You don't have to live guilty, feeling unworthy, afraid of what someone will say. God has you covered. Get back in the game. There's not a mistake you've made that has stopped your purpose. You may hear the hoofbeats of Pharaoh's army, the past chasing you, reminding you of the hurts, trauma, and mistakes, but all that is headed to the Red Sea. God has taken care of every threat, every mistake, every injustice. The negative things in your past are dead. What was trying to stop you is done. Now you have to do your part and go back to Egypt. Go back to dreaming, go back to loving the people God has given you. Go back to believing you are worthy. Go back to living with passion, with faith, with expectancy. You don't have time to waste being a prisoner of your past. You have a destiny to fulfill. There's a calling on your life.

If Moses had gotten stuck in the past, he would never have delivered the Israelites, never parted the Red Sea, never seen manna in the desert, never had water out of a rock. The best part of his life happened after a failure, after he had spent years hiding from his past. Who knows where God will take you if you'll go back to Egypt, if you quit running from your past, dwelling on your hurts, reliving the trauma, hiding your gifts. Your past was cleared, not in the Red Sea, but on the cross of Christ two thousand years ago. All those who were trying to harm you—that's done. There's a rainbow in the sky. There's not going to be another flood. There's no use building a tower, building walls, building defenses, planning for more trauma. Why don't you receive God's mercy, receive His forgiveness and cleansing? You may have had some ashes, but God has beauty coming. Pharaoh may have chased you through the Red Sea, but there's a promised land awaiting you.

I know your trauma was real, the injustice, the betrayal. I'm not making light of that. But you have to be aware of the enemy's schemes. He would love to use that to convince you to shrink back as Moses did and spend years hiding your gifts, living in regrets, being afraid of what might happen. It's time to come out of hiding. The best part of your life is still in front of you. You wouldn't be alive if God didn't have greater victories in your future. Guilt, shame, fear, trauma, and insecurity have to go. Those strongholds—those negative words people have spoken over you—are coming down. They don't define you. God's power in you is stronger and He will break every bondage from your past right now.

CHAPTER NINE

Declare Victory and Expect Favor

No person, no circumstance, no hurt or loss has the power to limit you and make you a victim. Our God is a God of justice, and He's not going to just bring you out of all the negative things that have happened; He's going to bring you out a victor.

We all go through things that are unfair. We can't do anything great; just look at how we were raised. We can't love again; the last person hurt us. We can't live happy; we've been through too much. As long as you accept that you're a victim, you're going to get stuck. You might have been through unfair situations, but don't use it as an excuse to feel sorry for yourself, to give up on life, to not pursue your dreams. Declare victory and expect favor, instead.

My mother had polio as a child. One of her legs was much smaller than the other. As a little girl, she had to wear a brace and couldn't run and play like the other children. She could have lived as a victim. But I never heard her complain. She never saw herself as being at a disadvantage. She went on to live a full, blessed, favor-filled life. She was married for almost forty years, had five children, and one son is very good looking—it isn't Paul. None of that would have happened if she had seen herself as a victim. Nothing that's happened to you has stopped your destiny. It might have been painful when the person did you wrong and walked away, but they didn't ruin your life. They don't have that much power. If they could stop God's plan, they would be bigger than God. Don't let one bad break, one injustice, one difficult season, cause you to be sour and have a chip on your shoulder. You will gain strength as you declare victory and expect God's favor. Keep declaring God's promises, keep holding on to His truth, and before long, you'll step into the fullness of who He created you to be.

A VICTOR'S MENTALITY

When my father went to be with the Lord, I lost my best friend. I had worked with him day in and day out for seventeen years. We had traveled the world together and suddenly he was gone. I was tempted to think, *God, where are You? This isn't fair. Why did this happen?* When we go through loss and things we don't understand, that victim mentality will always come knocking on the door. Then we have to make a choice. Are we going to live bitter, discouraged, thinking we're a victim of our circumstances? That we're a victim of the loss, a victim of the unfair boss, a victim of the illness? Or are we going to believe that God is in control? That He's ordering our steps, that His plans for us are for good? Instead of having a victim mentality, switch over to a victor mentality.

Declare Victory and Expect Favor

That bad break is not how your story ends. The loss, the sickness, or the injustice is not going to limit the rest of your life.

God said in Isaiah, "I will pay you back double for the unfair things that have happened." It may be unfair, but God is a just God. He saw what happened, He knows who hurt you, what you lost, what you're struggling with. He's not going to just bring you out; He's going to bring you out better. Get rid of that victim mentality. Quit dwelling on who hurt you, what you lost. You're not a victim. Nobody can make you a victim. They can do things that are unfair, and you can go through things you don't like, through situations you don't understand, but none of that can force you to have a victim mentality. You have to give permission to become a victim. You have to make that choice. Don't allow that victim mentality to enter your thinking. When unfair things happen, thoughts will whisper, *Just your luck, another bad break. You're scarred now, and life will always be difficult.* That's when you have to dig down deep and say, "No thanks. I refuse to be a victim. I refuse to live bitter, angry, thinking I've been shortchanged.

> **You have to give permission to become a victim.**

I know God is still on the throne. I know He didn't bring me this far to leave me. What was meant for my harm, He's turning to my advantage."

KEEP BEING YOUR BEST

In Chapter Six, we saw how Joseph, as a teenager, was thrown into a pit and then sold as a slave by his own brothers. His dreams were shattered and his freedom lost. Now Joseph was working in Egypt for a man named Potiphar. In one sense, he was a victim of his brothers' jealousy, a victim of bad breaks. He had plenty of reasons to have a victim mentality, but Joseph didn't go there. He didn't sit around in self-pity; he didn't give up on life. He kept being his best, treating people right, believing that God was in control. Potiphar's wife falsely accused Joseph of a crime, and he was put in prison for something he didn't do, giving him another reason to have a chip on his shoulder. Now he was the victim of this lady who was dishonest. But in prison, Joseph kept

> *In prison, Joseph kept shining. Before long, he was put in charge of the whole prison.*

shining. Before long, he was put in charge of the whole prison.

One of his cellmates was Pharaoh's former butler, who had a dream one night that he didn't understand. Joseph interpreted the dream and told him that in three days he was going to be released and reinstated as Pharaoh's butler. All Joseph asked for in return was for the butler to put in a good word for him. Just as Joseph had said, the butler got out and went back to his position, but he forgot all about Joseph. Joseph had yet another reason to feel like a victim. Thirteen years after he was originally thrown into the pit by his brothers, Joseph was called to the palace and interpreted a dream for Pharaoh. He so impressed Pharaoh that Pharaoh made him the prime minister of Egypt, his second-in-command.

During those thirteen years, practically every day Joseph had to fight having a victim mentality. Thoughts would whisper, *Look at where you are. You've done the right thing, and all these bad breaks have happened. Your own family turned on you, that lady lied about you, the butler forgot about you. It's never going to change. Just accept it.* But Joseph's attitude was: *I refuse to be a victim. I am not a victim of my brothers' jealousy. I'm not a victim of the lady who lied about me. I'm not a victim of the butler who's forgotten about me. They did me wrong, but God said He would make it up to me. They forgot about me, but God remembers me. They tried to push me down, but I know that God will lift me up.*

What's interesting is that God had a plan that made good things from all the bad breaks, all the betrayals, and the rejection. That's what led Joseph to see his dream come to pass. If he had seen himself as a victim, he would have missed his destiny. If he had been bitter about his brothers, angry over Potiphar's wife, in self-pity because the butler forgot about him, we wouldn't be talking about Joseph. This didn't happen automatically. He refused to be a victim. He refused to let his mind rehearse all the negative things. He refused to live with a chip on his shoulder. He didn't give permission to a victim mentality. I wonder where you will be in five years if you keep refusing to be a victim. I wonder how far God will take you if you just not live bitter over who hurt you, not try to get revenge on the friend who did you wrong, not lose your passion because you're dealing with an illness, not give up on your dreams because a door closed and it didn't happen the way you thought. Every voice will say, "You're a victim. Come on, accept it. It's not fair. God has forgotten about you." Don't give it the time of day.

God is watching you. He sees you shaking off the self-pity, doing the right thing when it's hard, being good to people who weren't good to you, giving it your best when you're not seeing progress. Your time is coming. Suddenly doors are going to open, suddenly the right people will show up, suddenly you'll see promotion, vindication, dreams coming to pass bigger than you've imagined.

BREAK THE FOREVER-THE-VICTIM CYCLE

When we say we're a victim, we're saying, "What someone did to me has limited my future." People don't have that kind of power over you. Circumstances cannot stop what God has ordained for your life. The Scripture says, "What God has purposed who can annul?" The only way it will stop you is if you start living as a victim, living discouraged and in self-pity. Shake that off. Those disappointments, the betrayal, or the closed door is setting you up for double. God saw the

> *Circumstances cannot stop what God has ordained for your life.*

person who succeeded in making you look bad, and you didn't get the promotion. It was a part of His plan. It's setting you up for something bigger than you've imagined.

Joseph could have been bitter after his brothers threw him into the pit. That wasn't fair, but it was a step on the way to his destiny. What you can't see is that that bad break is leading you to a new level. Potiphar's wife falsely accused Joseph and caused him to be put in prison. Joseph didn't understand it at the time, but that was a necessary step to get him to the throne. We're not going to understand everything that happens along the way. There will be plenty of opportunities to be a victim. These are tests. Will you keep the right attitude when it's not fair, when you feel discouraged? "Why did this happen?" No, refuse to be a victim. Don't play that role. It might have been meant for your harm, but at some point, as with Joseph, God is going to turn it to your advantage. It's going to catapult you to where you can't go on your own.

I met a young couple from New Orleans. They had just bought their first house there and were excited. The husband had a good job and was moving up in his company. They had a little baby on the way, their first child. Life was good, then the storm Katrina hit. It wiped out their whole neighborhood. They lost not only their house but all their possessions, their car, their clothes. His company closed, and he didn't have a job. They moved to Houston with just the clothes on their back. When I saw them, they were numb. Their whole world had fallen apart. Everything in their thinking said, *You're victims. Just accept it. Life will never be what it could have been.* I told them what I'm telling you, that God knows what you've been through. He's seen the tears you've shed, the heartache you've felt. He's not going to just bring you out, He's going to make the enemy pay. But you must do your part and refuse to be a victim. Refuse to live bitter, in self-pity, thinking you've seen your best days.

> *As long as you're playing the role of victim, you're giving the enemy permission to keep you defeated.*

I could see faith begin to rise in their hearts. Week after week, they kept coming to Lakewood hearing about how God is fighting our battles. Several years later, I met them after a service. They had just moved into their new house that they had built here. The man has a better job, with better income, less travel. They don't just have one child; they have two children. They said, "Joel, we never dreamed we could be where we are today." That's what happens when you refuse to be a victim. When you say "no thanks" to bitterness, "no thanks" to self-pity, "no thanks" to living defeated, God will take what was meant for harm and turn it to your advantage. But as long as you're playing the role of victim, you're giving the enemy permission to keep you defeated.

You may have come from generations of abuse, mistreatment, things that were not fair. That victim mentality can be passed from generation to generation. "We've always been poor, defeated, shortchanged. Look what we've been through. We have a good reason to feel like victims." This forever-the-victim mentality will try to take root. It will continue to be passed down until someone rises up and puts an end to it. Yes, there was injustice in the past; yes, there were things that were not fair; but this is a new day. The reason you're reading this is because you're the one to break the cycle, you're the one to say, "I am not a victim, I am a victor. I'm going to set a new standard. I'm going to believe for better things. I'm going to live whole, free, expecting favor."

VICTORY STARTS IN YOUR THINKING

The Israelites were in slavery for ten generations. All they knew was hardship, mistreatment, working long hours with no pay. It wasn't fair, but God was keeping the records. After 430 years, God delivered them from Pharaoh and brought them out of Egypt. You can imagine how they had become comfortable being a victim. It's all they had known. Their parents and their grandparents were all slaves, all mistreated. On the way to the Promised Land, when they faced adversity and heavy opposition, they said to Moses, "Let's go back to Egypt. Let's go back to being slaves." They were saying, "We're okay with being a victim. That's normal to us. That's what we're used to." They came out of Egypt, but Egypt never came out of them.

What's interesting is that when they were leaving Egypt, God caused the Israelites to have favor with their oppressors, who gave them their gold, silver, and fine clothing. They didn't leave empty-handed. God paid them back for 430 years of working for free. In Exodus 3, God told them what to do with the gifts they received. He said, "You are to dress your sons and daughters in this jewelry and fine clothing." Why would God have them get their children dressed up when they were about to go into the desert? It's because God wanted these children to see themselves differently. They saw themselves as slaves, as victims, like their parents—poor, defeated, limited. God knew if they were going to go into the Promised Land, they had to get rid of that victim mentality. He didn't have the parents put on the nice clothes or have the grown-ups wear the fine jewelry. He wanted to change the image of these small children.

> *God knew if they were going to go into the Promised Land, they had to get rid of that victim mentality.*

I can imagine a mother putting a gold necklace on her little daughter, whose face would brighten up like never before. A father put a ring on his son, who put his shoulders back, feeling so special. These children had worn raggedy old hand-me-down clothes; now the parents were dressing them in beautiful dresses, nice clean outfits. For the first time these children began to see themselves as victors. It's significant that the parents and grandparents never made it into the Promised Land. It's because they

Declare Victory and Expect Favor

never got rid of their victim mentality. They never quit seeing themselves as anything but poor, at a disadvantage. These children had a different mindset. It started when they put on the new clothing, the nice jewelry. Something shifted in their thinking. They thought, *Maybe we're not victims. Maybe we're not always going to struggle. Maybe we can live an abundant life.*

Victory starts in your thinking. As long as you feel like a victim, it's going to limit your destiny. You won't pray bold prayers, you won't believe for big dreams, and you won't expect God's favor. No matter what's happened in your past, no matter how many generations there's been of dysfunction, abuse, lack, and struggle, you're the generation that's going to set a new standard. You're the one who's going to see this shift in your thinking. *I am not a slave, I am not a victim, limited, or at a disadvantage. I am a child of the Most High God.*

> **No matter what's happened in your past, no matter how many generations there's been of dysfunction, abuse, lack, and struggle, you're the generation that's going to set a new standard.**

No more forever-the-victim. No more, "I always get bad breaks. It's just my luck." No more, "My family has always struggled. It's just who we are." God is doing a new thing. Now do your part and put on those new clothes, so to speak. See yourself differently. Have a new perspective. You're not a victim of your past, not a victim of who went before you, not a victim of what didn't work out. You are a victor. God is about to release freedom, wholeness, abundance, and favor like you've never seen. You've been raised up for such a time as this to make a difference, to take your family to a new level.

FOREVER-THE-VICTOR

There was a young woman in California who was riding her mountain bike on the trails of a state park as she had done many times before. As she was speeding down the mountainside, she noticed a blur out of the corner of her eye. She thought it was a deer, but it was a mountain lion leaping toward her. It knocked her to the ground, bit her face, and wouldn't let go. All she could do was whisper "Jesus!" Her friend threw her bike at the mountain lion, but it kept dragging her all the way to a ravine.

She thought she was done and passed out. When she woke up, she was in the hospital. Miraculously, her life was spared, although half of her face was disfigured. She had forty bite marks across her body, with two hundred staples holding her skin together. She had to have six surgeries to repair the damage. Everyone referred to her as "the victim of the mountain lion." That's true in one sense, but she was so much more than that. Negative things may have happened, but don't let what you've been through become your identity. Don't become known as the person who went through the tragedy, the person who lost their loved one, the man who lost his job. That's what happened to you; that's not who you are.

> **Negative things may have happened, but don't let what you've been through become your identity.**

When this young lady got out of the hospital, she told her friends that she wanted to go back to the trail where she was attacked. They were surprised and asked why. She said, "I'm not going to be a prisoner of this drama. I'm not going to let what's happened to me define who I am and cause me to live angry, bitter, and afraid." She was saying, "I'm not going to be forever-the-victim. This incident is not going to ruin the rest of my life." Today, she's healthy, free, moving forward, raising her children. We all have these opportunities to become a forever victim. We can't get past it. "It was too traumatic. They hurt me too badly. This disappointment is too painful, this loss too much." That's when you have to do as she did and say, "I refuse to be the victim. I refuse to let this limit my passion or cause me to give up on my dreams." That's what allows God to pay you back for the wrongs, to bring beauty out of the ashes, to give you double for the unfair things.

This is a choice we have to make all through life. It's not whether the hurts come or if you have bad breaks. These things are going to happen. The question is, are you going to live in self-pity and be bitter? Or are you going to say, "God, this wasn't fair, but I know You're still on the throne. It was a bad break, but You say You will pay me back. They did me wrong, but You're my vindicator. I'm going to trust You and move forward with my life"? Don't get stuck in the desert like the Israelites because you have a victim mentality. Be like their children and put on a new attitude, see yourself a different way, so you can go into your Promised Land. This is a new day. No more forever-the-victim. Try a different approach: forever-the-victor. Break the negative cycle.

Where will you be in five years if you start refusing to be the victim? This is not going to happen easily. Your feelings will want to feel sorry for yourself. This is when you have to be bold and refuse to be the victim. Refuse to play that role. That's not your part. Every unfair thing that's happened to you has set you up for double. God saw it, and He's promised to pay you back. Now do your part and play the right role, be the victor. If you do, like with Joseph, God will turn what was meant for your harm to your advantage. Like the Israelite children, you're going to go into your Promised Land, with promotion, restoration, vindication, healing, freedom, and abundance coming.

> *Where will you be in five years if you start refusing to be the victim?*

CHAPTER TEN

Let Your Light Shine

When God breathed His life into you, He didn't just put gifts, dreams, creativity, and potential for you alone; it's meant for you to share with the world. It's time to let your light shine and step into who God created you to be.

God has put gifts and talents in you. He's given you dreams and goals that are unique to your life. You have something to offer that nobody else has. But it's easy to let fear hold us back—fear of failure, fear of what people are going to think, fear of the unknown. "What if I try it and it doesn't work? What if people don't accept me? What if I don't have the talent?" Too often we let the what-ifs talk us out of it. Many people are living with hidden dreams, hidden talent, hidden potential. They've discounted themselves, thinking they're not as talented as their friends, they've had too many setbacks, they tried and failed in the past. All throughout these chapters, I've been encouraging you to rediscover the amazing person God created you to be. When you let your light shine, you're stepping into His plan, building the mindset to take back the life you were meant to live, and walking boldly into your God-given destiny.

My message is very simple: Don't hide what God has placed inside you—your gifts, your creativity, your heart. You may face setbacks, but don't shrink back in fear. Remember, God can't restore what you keep hidden. Step out, shine your light, and watch Him bring healing, strength, and favor into your life.

The Scripture says, "You don't light a candle and hide it under a bushel." When God breathed His life into you, He lit your candle. He created you to shine, to make a difference, to leave your mark. Your gift isn't just for you; it's to share with the world. We need your talent, we need your creativity, we need your smile. Stop telling yourself that you can't do it, it's too big, you're not talented enough, you don't have the experience. Stop pushing down that forgotten part of yourself that used to dream big dreams. Let your light shine!

God wouldn't have given you that dream if He had not equipped you. Don't let fear talk you out of it. You can't play it safe your whole life and become who God created you to be. He will put you in situations on purpose that look too big, too overwhelming. It's because He knows what's in you. He created you. He knows what you're capable of. Deep down you know you're supposed to step out, you know that gift is in you to do it, but maybe you're afraid, you feel unqualified, you don't have the training. You'll be tempted to stay in the boat and hide your gift. But if you take that step of faith, God will step in and help you do what you couldn't do. That gift will come to life, and you'll discover ability that you didn't know you had. But here's the key: You can't wait until the fear goes away and then you'll do it. "When I get my courage up, I'll teach the class, or I'll start my business, or I'll go out on that date." The fear may not go away. You're going to have to do it in spite of the fear. That's what faith is all about. "I feel afraid, but fear is not going to control my life. I'm going to step out in faith." Nobody who's ever done anything great in life has done it without fear. You will feel the fear, but you have to do it afraid.

> *You can't wait until the fear goes away and then you'll do it.*

I wish I could tell you that when you get close to taking that step of faith and releasing your gift that you will suddenly turn into another person and be full of courage, power, strength, and not feel any fear. But it may be just the opposite. You may feel more fear than ever. That's the enemy trying to deceive you into keeping your gift hidden. He doesn't want you to step into a new level. He doesn't want you to shine and go where no one in your family has gone or take new ground for the kingdom. He'll work overtime to try to convince you to shrink back and play it safe. You have to have a boldness that you are going to do it in spite of the fear.

"But what if I fail?" You get up and try again. Every failure is preparing you. You can't be so afraid of failure that you don't get out of your comfort zone. You will learn more through failure than you will through success. You'll learn more in the difficult times when it doesn't work out than you will in the good times. Thomas Edison failed ten thousand times before he finally invented the light bulb. A reporter asked him about all his failures. He said, "I never failed. I just learned ten thousand ways a light bulb wouldn't work." Even when it doesn't work out, you're learning, you're growing, you're one step closer to seeing it happen.

> *You will learn more through failure than you will through success.*

When we come to the end of life, nothing will be more disappointing than to think, *What would have happened if I had taken that step of faith? What could I have become if I didn't let fear hold me back? Where would I be if I wouldn't have hidden my talent, hidden my dreams, hidden my gifts?* Life is short. Stir up what God put in you. Make the most of every day.

Don't let the fear of failure, fear of what people are going to think, or fear of being criticized hold you back.

RELEASE YOUR GIFTS

One of the best things I've learned is that everybody is not supposed to be for you, everybody is not supposed to like you. You can't reach your destiny without opposition, without criticism, without negative chatter. We saw how Joseph wouldn't have made it to the throne without his brothers betraying him. David would never have become king without Goliath. Quit worrying about who's not for you. Some enemies are designed as a part of your destiny. They're not going to stop you; they're going to promote you. Keep running your race, not looking to the left or to the right. Remember, people can't make you feel inferior without your permission. You can't control what is said to you, but you can control your response. Don't be bothered by who's not for you, who's not cheering you on, and who's not celebrating you. You'll never please everyone. You can't keep all your friends, relatives, and coworkers happy. If you try, the one person who won't be happy is you. Other people may not see your gift. They don't know what God has put in you. They can't feel what you feel. Don't let their discouragement talk you out of it. Don't let the fear of what they think hold you back. You're not going to give an account to people of what you did with your life; you're going to give an account to God.

I wouldn't be doing what I'm doing today if I had not learned to step out even though I felt afraid. Are you letting fear hold you back? Are you hiding your gifts, hiding your talents, hiding your personality? Are you afraid to come out of your shell because you may not be accepted? It's time to let your light shine. Quit hiding your smile. Brighten others' day. Quit hiding your encouragement and lift somebody up. Quit hiding your talent and make the world better. If God has given you the gift to sing, start singing. If you can write, start writing. If you can lead, start leading. If you can build, start building. If you can teach, start teaching. God didn't give you those

> *Are you afraid to come out of your shell because you may not be accepted? It's time to let your light shine.*

gifts and talents to stay hidden. It doesn't do you any good, and it's not doing anyone else any good, if you keep it to yourself. It has to be released. He's expecting you to bring it out and develop it, to pursue it, to cultivate it. We have a responsibility to release what He has given us. Don't take it lightly. Don't live passively, just accepting what life brings your way. Shake off the complacency and get focused.

What could you accomplish if you weeded out things that are not moving you toward your destiny? Where could you be at this time next year if you got rid of the distractions and things that are not producing good fruit? What if you put all your efforts into the main thing that you know God put in your heart? It may mean taking a class online, getting things lined up to start the business, or finding a mentor whom you can learn from to develop your skills. You may be able to do many things well, but you can't do many things great. Sometimes we're too spread out. The apostle Paul says, "This one thing I do." Find that one thing and excel at it. Studies show when a person spends ten thousand hours doing the same thing, they become an expert. Find that one thing and do it to the best of your ability. That is how you let your light shine.

DEVELOP WHATEVER GIFT YOU HAVE

Too often we discount ourselves, thinking we don't have much to offer. We look at what we don't have and what we can't do. Your gift may seem small, but if you start using it, it will grow. It's like an acorn. You could look at it and think, *Big deal. All I have is this little gift. God, You created the universe, and this is all You've given me.* What you can't see is there is incredible potential in that small gift. In that little acorn is a huge oak tree, branches spreading out fifty feet wide. Don't discount your gift because it seems small. You could be praying for something that you already have. You just don't realize it.

> *Your gift may seem small, but if you start using it, it will grow.*

As a teenager out in the shepherds' fields, David could have thought, *God, all I'm good at is slinging rocks with this sling. Three of my brothers are in the military. They're big, strong, and talented. How come you didn't give me more talent?* Instead, David kept developing that small gift. Every day out in the fields, instead of being lazy and complaining about what he didn't have, he kept practicing, getting better with his sling. He could hit a bull's-eye a hundred feet away. One day he faced Goliath, a giant wearing armor that covered every part of his body except around his eyes and forehead. David picked up a stone and slung it, just as he'd practiced thousands of times, and it hit Goliath right in the forehead, right where there wasn't any armor. David became an instant national hero.

Your gift may seem small, but when you develop it, big doors will open. You don't have to have a great gift for God to use you in a great way. Proverbs 18:16 says, "A man's gift will make room for him." It doesn't say if you have a big gift, an important gift, an impressive gift. Whatever you have, if you develop it and keep getting better, it will open doors of opportunity, doors of promotion, doors of influence. Sometimes we're wondering why we're not being blessed, why we're not seeing increase. It's because we've buried our blessing, we've buried our promotion, we've

> *Whatever you have, if you develop it and keep getting better, it will open doors of opportunity, doors of promotion, doors of influence.*

buried our talent. It's time to dig up what's been hidden. Start releasing what's in you.

NO MORE DISCOUNTING YOURSELF

In John 6, Jesus was teaching thousands of people in a remote area. Late in the day, the people were tired and hungry. Jesus told His disciples to feed the people, but the only available food was five barley loaves and two fish that a young boy had brought. When the disciples had asked if anyone had any food, the boy could have thought, *The disciples don't need the little I have. It won't even make a dent in this huge crowd.* He could have discounted what he had and hid his lunch. But instead he gave it to the disciples, and Jesus blessed his lunch and it multiplied, feeding the five thousand men, besides women and children, who had gathered.

Your gift may seem small, but when you release it, it will multiply. As long as you hide it, as long as you keep it buried, it will be two fish and five loaves. You'll never see your potential until you release it. What are you hiding—gifts, dreams, creativity? Have you convinced yourself that it's too small, that you don't have the talent, that you could never do something significant? If you quit discounting what you have and start releasing it, God will multiply your influence, multiply your resources, multiply your talent.

I didn't have a big gift when my father went to be with the Lord. Compared to the need for a new pastor for Lakewood, it seemed insignificant. The church had six thousand people coming every Sunday. It was a megachurch. In the natural, we needed a mega pastor, with mega experience and mega talent, and I was none of those. But God doesn't choose the way we choose. He doesn't always go find the smartest, most gifted, most experienced. Many times, He will take what seems small and multiply it. That's what God did with me. I said, "God, this is all I have, just five loaves and two fish." It's not how much you have; it's what you are doing with what you have. Have you buried it because you are intimidated, afraid, insecure? Why? You're a child of the Most High God. You've been crowned with favor. You have seeds of greatness. I'm asking you to get that dream out, get

> *It's not how much you have; it's what you are doing with what you have.*

that gift out, and start releasing it and watch what God will do. He'll take you where you could not go on your own. He'll exceed your expectations.

It's time to step into who God created you to be. Your gifts, your talents, and your dreams have been buried long enough. You have greatness in you. There are talents that you haven't discovered. As you take steps of faith, God will make things happen that you couldn't make happen. Don't bury your talent; bury your fears and release your talent. Live faith-based, not fear-based. If you do this, like the little boy with the lunch, what you're releasing is going to multiply. You're going to accomplish dreams that look impossible. Talent is going to come out that you didn't know you had, doors are going to open that you couldn't open. You're going to rise higher, overcome obstacles, shine brighter, and reach the fullness of your destiny.

An Invitation for Further Reflection

Chapter One Reflections: Rediscover the Forgotten You

1. Some people look in the mirror and wonder where the outgoing, joyful, confident, passionate person has gone. Have you found this to be true in your life as well? Take some time to reflect on your experience and describe what you feel you've lost.
2. In spite of whatever you may have lost, what good news does God have for you? What was your immediate response when you read this? Do you believe it is possible?
3. Read Genesis 3:1–11. Has there been a time in your life when God asked you, as He asked Adam, "Where are you?" What do you think He was really asking you? How did you respond?
4. Because of what we've gone through, we tend to go into hiding and to isolate. Describe one area of your life that you are hiding and what it was that

caused you to isolate it. Why is it so damaging to keep it hidden?

5. The enemy tells us lies to convince us that we're not valuable, not up to par, at a disadvantage, a failure. Name some of the lies that have affected your self-image and confidence and caused you to shrink back. How do you quit giving those lies permission to determine your worth and value?

6. God also asked Adam, "Who told you that you were naked?" Why is it so important to identify the source of negative thoughts and emotions? How do you deal with the lies that come to deceive you into hiding who you are?

7. Read 1 Kings 18–19. What valuable lesson does the prophet Elijah's story tell? What did God tell him he needed to do? What is the still small voice saying to you?

Chapter Two Reflections: Believe In the True You

1. How does Psalm 139:13–15 describe the true you? How wonderfully has God made you? When life experiences bring flaws, insecurity, shame, and guilt, what is the good news that you need to remember?

2. In what ways was Michelangelo's sculpting of the marble statue of King David similar to the way God is working to make you into His masterpiece? What vision does He have of you? What are some specific ways God is working on you now?
3. Sometimes when God chisels to remove something from our life, it's uncomfortable. Describe some times when God removed something that you couldn't understand. Did you fight the chisel? Looking back, why do you think He removed what He did?
4. When other people look at you, what flaws do you think they see in you, and how does that cause them to treat you? Why do your flaws not influence God's view of you?
5. Read Luke 5:1–11. What can you learn from Peter's experience of feeling so unworthy of being with Jesus? What did Jesus see in Peter, and what did he become? What encouragement does this give you?
6. Are there people in your life who have tried to discount you and tell you what you can't become? Describe what you've faced. What is the truth about what other people think about you?

7. What have you learned in this chapter about what God is doing in your life and how He is doing it? Write a summary of your thoughts.

Chapter Three Reflections: Change Your Name

1. How have you been letting people and circumstances put names on you? What are those names? Have you accepted those names into your thinking?
2. Who do you believe you are? How do you see yourself? Reflect on the names that your own thoughts regularly label you. How do those names impact how you speak, act, and react?
3. Read Genesis 35:16–18. Describe the contrast between the names Ben-Oni and Benjamin. Have some people who should have been speaking faith over your life done just the opposite? Describe your experience.
4. Are you answering to names that you're not? Are you letting those names get in you? What are the names that you should be answering to? Write a list of the names that describe who God says you are.
5. What valuable lesson can you take from the naming of Erwin McManus by his grandfather? How

powerful was that name? How powerful are the names God gives you?
6. Read Genesis 17. Why did God change the names of Abram and Sarai? What difference did it make? Name one troublesome area of your life where you will start calling yourself by what God has named you. What happens every time you do that?
7. There is always going to be a "they" who tries to name you what you're not. Based on what you have learned in this chapter, write a summary of how you are going to accept God's name changes and align your thoughts accordingly.

Chapter Four Reflections: Build Yourself Up

1. What is the problem with relying on others to make you feel valued and appreciated? Describe some instances when your reliance on others led to disappointments.
2. The Scripture says, "Build yourselves up in your most holy faith" (Jude 1:20). How do you do that? In what specific ways do you need to start doing that today?
3. What does John 7:38 mean? Have you recognized that it is true in your life? In what ways do you, and in what ways have you not?

4. Reflect on the thought from Genesis 1 that God approved and celebrated His work after every day of creation. What does His example tell you about His work in your life? What encouragement does knowing this give you?
5. You should be for yourself, approving yourself, not against yourself. On a scale of 1 to 10, with 1 being against yourself and 10 being for yourself, how would you grade yourself? Explain why you think that.
6. Describe a time when the external approval and applause you were receiving from others stopped unexpectedly. How did you respond? Knowing what you do now, how would you respond differently?
7. Today can be a turning point for you. Write a declaration that you are no longer going to live dependent on others for your approval and self-worth as well as the changes in your thinking that will make that happen.

Chapter Five Reflections: Get Your Mind Going in the Right Direction

1. Read Galatians 5:17. Describe the battle between the flesh and the spirit that is going on in your life. Which side is winning at the moment?

2. The apostle Paul says, "If you live according to the flesh, you will die; but if by the Spirit you put to death the deeds of the body, you will live" (Romans 8:13). When you let the flesh rule, what does your life look like? How do you put that to death by the Spirit?
3. Read Hebrews 12:11. Name five areas of your life where you know you need to exercise discipline in order to rule over the old you. How will you start to starve the temptations and negatives that try to control you?
4. What valuable lesson can you take from how David battled and defeated his personal enemies? Are there personal battles you're not dealing with that are keeping you from your best? What are some steps you can take this week to change that?
5. Some personal enemies are defeated easily and quickly, while others are stubborn like Saul and are not removed. Do you understand what your real enemy is and where your real battle lies? What must you guard against?
6. God changed the name of Jacob, which means "deceiver," to Israel, which means "prince with God," yet on some occasions he still was referred to as Jacob. What does this tell you about your

own conflict between the old you and the new you? How do you keep the old you in the grave?
7. What is the lesson of the threshing process? What was the outcome of this process in Peter's life? Write a statement of the outcome you want to see in your life.

Chapter Six Reflections: Stand Strong as God's Masterpiece

1. When we go through unfair situations, when we're not treated right, when people walk away, we can lose who we are. Take some time now and write an honest review of some of the ways you have let your environment determine your identity.
2. Read Genesis 39. How did Joseph's environment contradict what God promised him? When you're in a negative environment, how does Joseph's example show you how to guard your true identity?
3. What never changed as Joseph went through one bad circumstance after another? What does that say about the difficulties that look permanent in your life? How does that encourage your faith?
4. If James Earl Jones were here today, what do you think he would tell you if you're letting fear, guilt,

shame, intimidation, and weaknesses convince you to live hiding your gifts, hiding what God put in you?
5. How do you stop looking into the distorting mirror with its wrong images of you and rediscover the real you? When what you see is only a negative story, how do you not get talked out of who you know you are and what God has for you?
6. The prophet Samuel anointed David to be the next king of Israel, but he went back to the shepherds' fields rather than to the palace. What is God showing you about seasons when you feel stuck? How do you keep yourself encouraged in those situations?
7. What powerful message did young Steve Harvey receive from his father that kept alive a dream that a teacher's words nearly crushed? How do you keep your dream alive when your circumstances contradict it?
8. What graphic terms were used by the ten spies that defined their present identity when they said it was impossible to conquer the Promised Land? How do you see your identity now at the close of this chapter? How do you keep from falling into the trap of the ten spies?

Chapter Seven Reflections: Know That You Are Destined for Greatness

1. Have you ever had a moment when you knew God was speaking to your heart and telling you who you are, His prized possession, His masterpiece, His child? Describe that moment. How has it impacted your life?
2. Read Judges 6. What was Gideon's identity when the angel spoke to him in the winepress? Facing what looked like an impossible circumstance, how did Gideon rediscover his true identity?
3. Abraham and Sarah had a promise from God for a son, but what mistake did they make that was similar to Gideon's mistake?
4. Do you find yourself praying for God to send someone to do something to bring change to your family or your circumstances? What are you asking for? What if you are the answer to your prayer? Are you discounting yourself?
5. What valuable lesson can you take from Todd Price's story? How is his story similar to your story? What doors might God open for you that you've not dreamed possible?
6. Read 2 Samuel 9. Who was Mephibosheth? Contrast his true identity with his identity in Lo

Debar. What was the key to Mephibosheth rediscovering all that he had lost?
7. Write down the top three challenges to your true identity that you are facing right now in your present circumstances. Then write a declaration of how knowing what it means to be a child of God will help you overcome what seems insurmountable.

Chapter Eight Reflections: Forget the Past, Focus on the Future

1. We've all had negative experiences that have left scars and regrets that try to keep us trapped in the past. Describe something you've gone through that you've felt you have to keep hidden but is keeping you from moving forward.
2. How does the apostle Paul's life demonstrate that nothing in your past can stop your future? What would we be missing out on if it did? What does that say about your past?
3. Read Genesis 10:8–12; 11:1–5. Why is it thought that Nimrod built the Tower of Babel, and what was its purpose? What has research shown about the effect of past trauma on future generations?
4. Do you deal with certain tendencies or issues that you think have been passed down within

your family line? What are they, and why do you think that? What can you do about generational limitations?

5. What did God do about the construction on the Tower of Babel? What is God showing you through His intervention there? What type of tower should you be building instead?

6. Read Exodus 14. What powerful lesson can you take from the pursuit of the freed Israelite slaves by Pharaoh and his chariots? Do you hear some hoofbeats chasing you? Why do you not have to keep looking back and shrinking back?

7. What in Moses' past kept him in hiding for forty years? What did God say He had done to take care of that problem in Exodus 4:19? What was the outcome? Write a summary of what God has done with your past.

Chapter Nine Reflections: Declare Victory and Expect Favor

1. Have you gone through things that are unfair and been left feeling that you're a victim and disadvantaged? Are you stuck there? Are other people and situations so powerful that they can

stop your destiny or ruin your life? Explain your thoughts.
2. What does Isaiah 61:7 tell us that God will do when we've been treated unfairly? How does that break a victim mentality? What do you have to do to maintain a victor's mentality?
3. Describe the thirteen years that followed Joseph's being sold into slavery by his brothers. What was the only thing that kept Joseph moving forward from the pit to the palace? What do you have to do every time your thoughts tell you, "You're a victim here. Come on, accept it"?
4. Read Numbers 14:1–4. After the Israelites had been in slavery for ten generations, God delivered them and was leading them to the Promised Land. Why did they allow hardships to cause them to fail to go in? Explain what it means when it says, "Victory starts in our thinking."
5. Read Exodus 3:21–22. After all their mistreatment as slaves, what remarkable gift of favor did God provide the Israelites as they began the exodus? Why did God have the parents dress their children in these riches?
6. What lesson can you take from the young woman who was nearly killed by a mountain lion?

7. Based on what you have learned in this chapter, what changes in your thinking will help you live with a forever-the-victor mentality?

Chapter Ten Reflections: Let Your Light Shine

1. All throughout these chapters you've been encouraged to rediscover the amazing person God created you to be. Read Matthew 5:15. What does it mean to let your light shine, and what amazing thing happens when you do?
2. What gifts has God given you, and why did He give them? Has fear caused you to hide those gifts? What do you need to do to step out of what feels safe and let those gifts come to life?
3. What is the truth about failure? Have you recognized that it is true in your life? In what ways do you, and in what ways have you not?
4. What could you accomplish if you weed out the things in your life that are not moving you toward your destiny, the distractions from your purpose, things that are not producing good fruit? Take some time now and write a list of what holds you back.
5. How do you view the gift God has given you? Do you discount it as small and insignificant? Why?

What steps can you take to develop it and keep getting better?
6. Read John 6:1–15. What lesson can you take from the young boy who offered his lunch to the disciples? What will God do when you release your gifts, dreams, and creativity?
7. What are the major things that God has shown you through this book? Write a plan for how you will move on to the complete rediscovering of the forgotten you.

Acknowledgments

In this book I offer many stories shared with me by friends, members of our congregation, and people I've met around the world. I appreciate and acknowledge their contributions and support. Some of those mentioned in the book are people I have not met personally, and in a few cases, we've changed the names to protect the privacy of individuals. I give honor to all those to whom honor is due. As the son of a church leader and a pastor myself, I've listened to countless sermons and presentations, so in some cases I can't remember the exact source of a story.

I am indebted to the amazing staff of Lakewood Church, the wonderful members of Lakewood who share their stories with me, and those around the world who generously support our ministry and make it possible to bring hope to a world in need. I am grateful to all those who follow our services on television, podcasts, Joel Osteen on SiriusXM, and global digital platforms. You are all part of our Lakewood family.

I offer special thanks also to all the pastors across the country who are members of our Champions Network.

Once again, I am grateful for a wonderful team of professionals who helped me put this book together for you. Leading them is my FaithWords/Hachette publisher Daisy Hutton, whose guidance I have been so thankful for over the years, along with the team at FaithWords. I truly appreciate the editorial contributions of wordsmith Lance Wubbels, and a special thanks to Phil Munsey for his insights and friendship.

I am grateful also to my literary agents Jan Miller Rich and Shannon Marven at Dupree Miller & Associates.

And last but not least, thanks to my wife, Victoria, and our children, Alexandra and Jonathan and his wife, Sophia, who are my sources of daily inspiration. Thanks as well to our closest family members, who serve as day-to-day leaders of our ministry: my brother, Paul, and his wife, Jennifer; my sister Lisa and her husband, Kevin; and my brother-in-law Don and his wife, Jackelyn.

We Want to Hear from You!

Each week, I close our international television broadcast by giving the audience an opportunity to make Jesus the Lord of their lives. I'd like to extend that same opportunity to you. Are you at peace with God? A void exists in every person's heart that only God can fill. I'm not talking about joining a church or finding religion. I'm talking about finding life and peace and happiness. Would you pray with me today? Just say, "Lord Jesus, I repent of my sins. I ask You to come into my heart. I make You my Lord and Savior."

Friend, if you prayed that simple prayer, I believe you have been "born again." I encourage you to attend a good Bible-based church and keep God in first place in your life. For free information on how you can grow stronger in your spiritual life, please feel free to contact us.

Victoria and I love you, and we'll be praying for you. We're believing for God's best for you, that you will see your dreams come to pass. We'd love to hear from you!

We Want to Hear from You!

To contact us, write to:

Joel and Victoria Osteen
PO Box #4271
Houston, TX 77210

Or you can reach us online at joelosteen.com.

@JoelOsteen

Stay encouraged *and* inspired all through the week.

Download the Joel Osteen Daily Podcast and subscribe now on YouTube to get the latest videos.

SiriusXM **Spotify** **Apple Podcasts** **YouTube**

Joel Osteen
NETWORK

Experience faith and hope 24 hours a day, 7 days a week. **All Free-to-Watch**

Streaming now on

The Roku Channel · Xumo Play · MyFree DIRECTV

TABLO · local now · TCLtv+ · sling

VIZIO WatchFree+ · prime video · Comcast xfinity · Freeplay